The electric guitar is the most expressive musical instrument ever developed. When people started work on amplifying guitars a hundred years ago nobody foresaw its exciting future. They were simply trying to make sure it could be heard alongside other instruments. As the guitar was turned up louder unwanted effects like distortion and sonic feedback occurred. Later players learned to use those effects to their advantage, creating previously unheard of ways of making music. Combining a guitar with an electronic pickup and an amplifier was just the starting point for a revolution in music that saw the guitar eventually achieve musical dominance.

Marc Bernard
Guitarist - Portland Oregon

Charlie Christians ES-250, thanks to Lynn Cartwright

A CENTURY OF THE ELECTRIC GUITAR

Sid Bishop & David Plues

ISBN 978-1-57424-424-3
SAN 683-8022

Design - David Plues

P.O. Box 17878-Anaheim Hills, CA
www.Centerstream-USA.com

Thanks to our friend Ron Middlebrook at Centerstream who has supported and encouraged us throughout the project - we couldn't have done it without you....

Credits and thanks

This book would not have been possible without the help and encouragement from the many collectors, photographers, musicians and friends - all experts in their own fields. If we have missed anyone please accept our humble apologies.

Thanks Marc Bernard for the opening page

Special Thanks
Jacques Menach who provided the photos for the cover and many features throughout the book
Francesco Balossino (Cesco's Corner) - our 'go to' expert for Fender guitars
Rob Lurvey for his amazing collection
Craig Brody - who went the extra mile
John Hill (ex Fender) and Pat Foley (ex Gibson)
Raul Barrios - collector and photographer
Gary Dick for the opening montage photo
Peter and Gail Hoarty - Northern Guitar Shows
Thanks are due to David's wife Dorothy, and Sid's wife Marie, for their saintlike patience

Tom Wittrock, Bill Fajen, Benjamin Isaacs, Eliot Michael, Justin Harrison, Martin Taylor, Edward Lott, Maton Guitars, Mick Hogan, Neil Flemming, Simon White, Simon Gauf, Yoshi Aono, Roger Giffin, Mike at Conti guitars, Scott Beckwith, Vic DaPra, Mufasa Shu, Lyn Wheelright (Vintage Guitar Mag) William P Gottlieb, Guy Tarium, Guitar Village, ATB Guitars, Paul Brett, Rob Lawrence, Bob Hewitt, Well Strung Guitars, Viktor Nemeth, Kris Blakely, Arthur Ramm, Bob & Cal Wootton, Willie Smith, Mogens Pederson, Phils Vintage Guitars, John Shannon, Vintage & Rare Bath, James Liverani, Derek Bruneau Cosmo, Mark Chatfield, Frank Manno, Fred Stucky, Carter Vintage Guitars, Ford Thurston, Alan Clarke, Pete Thorn, David Hesketh, Eric Ernest, Paul Beardow, Jim Hilmar, Dave D'Amelio, Howard Paul Jed Johnson, Ash Gupta, Michael Schenker, George Berry, Dave Keeling, Matt Lucas

We offer our sincere condolences to the family of our good friend Pat Foley who was a great help during the writing of this book

We worked together on the third volume of Burst Believers and have remained firm friends and collaborators ever since. It was Sid's idea to write a book about the momentous effect the electric guitar has had on the musical community, and on modern culture more widely, since its arrival a remarkable 100 years ago. We have turned to a large number of experts, guitarists, and dedicated fans to create our homage to an instrument which has had such an impact on not merely the music we listen to, but to the society which clothes us all. The guitar, and the music it became capable of producing, ushered in a new age and spawned a sub-culture which left our parents and grandparents baffled. In our younger days teenagers had it all and if you played a guitar you were King Of The Hill.

David and Sid

Sid started playing guitar at the age of 14, and was in a pro band by the age of 20. Following that he worked for decades in the retail guitar trade, both in the UK and the US, and sold instruments to many of the most legendary names in rock history. In the 1970s, and under the name of Ian C. Bishop, he wrote two Gibson history books and witnessed the birth of the Vintage and Classic guitar market. He has written many articles for a variety of industry magazines reflecting his fascination for the instrument, its history, and evolution over the last 100 years.

David Plues began playing guitar at the age of 13, his heroes being Hank Marvin and Django Reinhardt. David has a special interest in vintage and steel guitars. He has had a long and varied professional career accompanied throughout by his beloved classic Epiphone Riviera. A prolific writer he has become best known for his writing of the much respected Burst Believers books, which examine the phenomenon of the original series of Gibson's sunburst Les Paul Standards, a further volume on the Gold Top Les Pauls, and the recent release of a book on Gibson's ES series. With a worldwide network of fans there is no better new project than to celebrate the centenary of the electric guitar.

thanks Gary Dick and photographer Benjamin Isaacs - Gary's Classic Guitars

Introduction

2028 marks the one hundredth year of the electric guitar. There were many vitally important inventions that impacted all of our lives during the 20th century, but this has to be one of the greatest, changing not just various aspects of popular culture, but also the entire landscape, or soundscape if you prefer, of the popular music that is the backdrop to all of our lives. There would have been no rock and roll without the raw dynamic of the electric guitar to drive it along, nor any of the other musical genres that emerged from that during subsequent decades. No Chuck Berry, no Jimi Hendrix, no B B King, no Eddie Van Halen, or scores of other virtuosos. What a bleak world it could have been, not to mention quieter.

The evolution and development of the electric guitar that we all love so much now has traveled a road one hundred years long, and a road full of potholes. New ideas have emerged, some of which have been successful and stood the test of time, whilst others, although they seemed good ideas at the time, were less popular, burned briefly, and sank without trace, and now are no more than fascinating footnotes in the instruments history. Many weird, wonderful, and unconventional body styles pop up now and again, particularly prevalent in today's heavy metal genre, and some of those have stubbornly persisted, and I'm thinking of the Gibson Flying V, the Gibson Explorer, the B C Rich, the Vox Teardrop (debatable), Gibson's Firebird and others, although the Gibson Corvus, the Burns Flyte, Ovation's Deacon and Breadwinner models, and Fender's Katana are somewhat less so. Some body styles seem to be the result of fashion, or possibly merely a brief fad, so don't hang around for long. Another factor is that most guitars, of all types, have traditionally been made of wood. Concerns have emerged about the rising prices of suitable timbers, and of dwindling supplies. Resulting from those concerns many manufacturers have investigated, and experimented with, alternative materials. We have recently seen fretboards made of synthetic materials and mother of pearl replaced by mother of plastic. There are designers who have used other materials for their own sake, for practicality, to lower production costs, or just because they look nice. If we cast our minds back to the '70s we might recall the Dan Armstrong guitars and basses with their lucite bodies, the Steinberger headless guitars, also made of plastic, the aluminum Veleno and the current instruments made by the Electrical Guitar Company, also made of aluminum. We also might recall those early Kramers with aluminum necks, and the Travis Bean with its central section, including the neck, pickups and bridge components, all mounted on a billet of aluminum. Ovation's acoustic guitars have their bodys' bowl shaped backs made from a plastic derived from the technology associated with the manufacture of helicopter blades. Danelectro guitars first appeared in 1954, and the premise was to produce a usable guitar at a very low price. To that end the company made a range of guitars and basses, with bodies that were made from two sheets of hardboard (known as Masonite in the US) which were attached to a simple guitar shaped wood frame. It worked and those guitars are with us to this day. Concerning timbers there is one other factor, and that is the CITES regulation, introduced in 1975. That stands for the Convention On International Trade In Endangered Species, and concerns the preservation of scarce timbers preventing the export of such things from country to country. This has hit the instrument trade particularly severely, and restricts the usage of previously commonly used timbers such as ebony, Brazilian rosewood or Honduras mahogany from being used. That is one factor that has driven manufacturers to find alternatives, which is why you are now seeing baked maple, which almost looks like rosewood, being used on fretboards, amongst other things. All pieces in the jigsaw puzzle however, and all part of the big picture. What I'm looking at here is to present a history of each individual guitar manufacturer. Only briefly will you be reading about how each company was founded, all of its mergers, bankruptcies, changes of ownership and buy outs. All of that information can readily be found elsewhere if you require it. What I'm looking at here are the guitars themselves, what led to their invention, and how they developed. The necessity for such an instrument as an amplified guitar was largely prompted by big band guitarists of the prewar period. They wanted to solo just like the trumpeters and saxophone players but found their acoustic guitars to be totally swamped by the blast from a brass section. Amplification of some kind was essential in order that they could lift themselves to the next level. Necessity is the mother of invention, as is often said.

Although this is endlessly debatable there is no single person, or company, that we can point to as the inventor of the electric guitar. The basic theory behind the concept had been known for some time, and tinkerers, inventors, musicians and electrical engineers were busily bent over benches in workshops, garages, and garden sheds all across America, and other countries too, in order to find a way that the theory could be put to practical use. The Oscar however must go to Stromberg, whose Electro guitar of 1928 became the first commercially available electric guitar, and that is the centenary that we celebrate in these pages. It was a simple, even primitive affair, just a round hole flat top acoustic with a steel rod that ran longitudinally through the body to which were attached piezo electric contact microphones, a principle later perfected by companies such as Barcus-Berry, Fishman, and many others. To be totally honest it wasn't much, but it was a start. I shouldn't think that the first electric toasters were very impressive either. In certain other ways 1928 was important too. Bo Diddley was born in that year. A seminal player of the guitar, he even gave his name to a particular style of playing, and a sound, which though much copied, was basically his own. 1928 also witnessed the first appearance of machine sliced and mechanically wrapped bread. What's better than sliced bread? I think you know the answer to that one.

In 1935 T-Bone became the first Blues guitarist to play the electric guitar. He moved to Los Angeles and would be a regular at The Trocadero Club in Hollywood, where he achieved star status. He was considered to be the father of electric blues and rock 'n' roll. Eddie Lang and Charlie Christian were the jazz players who brought the electric guitar to popularity but the Chicago blues players were the pivotal players which would bring about the electric guitar as we know it today.

Eddie Lang - the father of the modern day guitar

The evolution of the electric guitar has been closely built around players utilizing the inventions and developments of the time, everything from guitar design, electrics and pickups, amplifiers, recording techniques and effects. Eddie Lang was a sensational player who embraced everything around him to create interesting recordings. Without an electric guitar as such, he would close-mic the guitar to capture not only volume but tone and special effects. He was the first player to capture the attention of the public with his style of playing whether it was plectrum, fingers, single line jazz runs or chord melody. He used everything in the guitarists arsenal to make sensational recordings and many would follow his lead in the years to come.

He tragically died in 1933, on the cusp of the electric age, ending what would certainly have been a stellar career. He was just 30 years old.

THE BIG BROADCAST - Bing Crosby (center), Eddie Lang (right), 1932 - courtesy Alamy

We will illustrate the book with photos of many of the landmark and important instruments made over the past 100 years. The Stromberg of course, the early Rickenbackers, the ES150, Telecaster and Esquire, the Stratocaster the Gibson Les Paul and ES335, the Travis Bean, Kramer, Veleno, Dan Armstrongs with their lucite bodies, the Bond guitar, and right up to today's carbon fibre and aluminum examples. Then of course the Japanese enter the fray, and in a big way. I have the greatest respect for Japanese makers, they produce some very fine instruments, used by some of the world's leading players, although I don't think they added very much new, other than making them more cheaply. No innovations in my view. They basically copied American or European original designs and components. Numerically however, instruments made in various countries in the Far East dominated the market and continue to do so. Somewhat remarkably in the late '80s and into the '90s Korean manufacturer Samick made 80% of all the guitars in the world. Guitars, especially budget priced and entry level guitars, have been produced in Japan, South Korea, Taiwan, Vietnam and Indonesia. The Martin company bought a factory in India just a few years back. Latterly the Chinese, having the greatest capacity for output, and a vast supply of good quality yet cheap timbers, dominate the lower end of the market. In response the major American makers have either decided to make all of their guitars in the Far East, such as Gretsch and Guild, or make their own dedicated budget lines, such as Gibson's Epiphone range, or the Squiers made by Fender. Rickenbacker currently stand alone as being the only company to stand its ground against the temptation to outsource manufacture to Asia.

The next electric guitar appeared in 1931 and was the Rickenbacker (so called) Frying Pan. This was also the first solid body guitar and was manufactured from cast aluminum. It was also a lap style Hawaiian guitar, not a conventional "Spanish" instrument. Hawaiian music was massively popular in the '30s and '40s, and in fact right into the '50s, and this is where Rickenbacker, at that time, had determined where their biggest market existed. Production of lap steel guitars grew through the '30s but later models were in bakelite rather than aluminum. The guitar however featured an electromagnetic pickup, instantly superseding the earlier experimental contact types of pickup. The first electromagnetic pickup was invented by George Beauchamp and is the unit seen on the Frying Pan. It utilized two horseshoe shaped magnets which were mounted over the coil itself. The coil was beneath the strings, and wound around six iron slugs, the purpose of which was to focus the magnetic field to each string Most modern pickups have magnetic pole pieces, or in some cases blades, actually mounted within the coil itself, but the basic principle is the same. Beauchamp was himself a lap steel player, thus much of Rickenbacker's early output concentrated on that type of guitar, but Beauchamp also designed an electric Spanish style guitar. Development took a couple of years but the guitar was ready to market by 1935. He was a very clever man indeed, responsible for more than one giant leap forward in the development of the electric guitar. He certainly would have contributed much more had he not died in 1941 at the age of just 42. We owe him a great deal.

1933 Dobro All Electric
EL 3945

Stromberg Electro mid 1930
Thanks to Lyn Wheelright and
Vintage Guitar Magazine

thanks to Jacques Menache

Jerry Byrd JB Frying Pan 1935

The development of the electric guitar owed much to the popularity of the steel guitar in the pre-war era. The first pickups were manufactured especially for the steel guitar and a specialty was the introduction of matching guitars and amplifiers.
Popular players in the '30s were Jerry Byrd, Sol Hoopii and later in the '40s the UK player, Harrry Brooker whose authentic Hawaiian technique was respected world wide.

A collection of Rickenbacker and Gibson EH lap steel guitars
the Rob Lurvey collection

The first Epiphone electric was the Electar, launched in 1935, once again a lap steel, all the rage in the 1930s. Interestingly enough this instrument was the first to feature a pickup with adjustable pole pieces. Small screws could be raised or lowered to achieve a true string balance and cure the ever present issue of a preponderant B. This development was soon copied by almost every other pickup maker and is commonplace now. The first true Spanish style Epiphone appeared in 1939. The Epiphone company and Gibson, were arch rivals for decades, featuring ranges of very similar guitars and mandolins etc, but by the 1950s Epiphone were struggling badly, largely due to disputes within the family that owned the company and partly due to financial crises resulting from falling sales. The company was bought by Gibson in 1957, and from 1958 onwards all Epiphones were produced in the Kalamazoo factory alongside the twin Gibson models, including new ranges of Epiphone branded solid body guitars, early versions of which feature the so called New York pickups that had previously been fitted to guitars such as the Broadway, Regent and Triumph. In 1976 the then Gibson owners, Norlin, decided to move all Epiphone production to Japan. A wide variety of models have appeared since, and at present most production is carried out in China. The range concentrates on reissues of classic originals from the '50s and '60s, which is obviously what the market demands.

In the '30s there was a real war between Gibson and Epiphone and the Epi' brand had a great artist relationship which gave them a lead over their arch rival. This guitar was offered for sale from Kansas City Vintage Guitars and was typical of that time - an arch body with added pickup. World War II would disrupt the industry and when normality returned after 1945 Gibson would take the initiative and become the prominent manufacturer

A young Les Paul surrounded by the instruments of the day

Another inveterate tinkerer was Paul Bigsby. He had also become aware of the unquestionable benefits of solid body instruments, and his first solid body guitar was made in 1948, trumping Fender's by two years. It was made at the behest of country star Merle Travis. Bigsby went on to make many more guitars of various designs, including twin necks, but he is best remembered now due to his invention of the ubiquitous spring loaded vibrato unit, fitted to just about every single guitar you can think of.

CHARLIE CHRISTIAN

The very first Gibson electric, apart from a couple of lap steel models from 1935, was the ES150, the ES standing for Electric Spanish, which was made available in 1936. It was designated 150 as it cost $150. If it was released today it would likely be the ES 3150 following the same logic. It came with a small amplifier, not much bigger than the average lunchbox, which kicked out about 2 watts. Many people complained that it wasn't much louder than a banjo. It was fitted with a distinctive single bar style pickup that had previously featured on several of Gibson's lap steel guitars. The guitar became the instant favored guitar of Charlie Christian, a leading player of the day. That pickup became known as the Charlie Christian pickup. It still is. John Lennon had one fitted to his Les Paul Special. The ES range expanded exponentially as the years passed. It gave us the 125, 130, 225, 175, 350, and the three quarter scale ES140, aimed at the beginner. Gibson theorized that if you caught players early enough they would have brand loyalty for life. By 1958 the ES range included the 335, which together with its siblings, the 330, 345 and 355, and is one of the most popular and iconic guitars of all time.

What a thrill to play Charlie Christian's guitar (and amp) tonight at The Jazz Loft, Stony Brook, Long Island with Frank Vignola and Pasquale Grasso.
Martin Taylor August 2024

Charlie Christian has become legendary. He wrote the book on solo jazz guitar. Without his genius it is possible that the electric guitar would have been smothered almost at birth. That's how important he was. His style of playing was studied and emulated by both the great "West Coast" jazz players and the Chicago Blues men. The electric guitar was now a solo instrument enjoying equal footing with the traditional horn men. The electric guitar revolution had got under way and there was no stopping it.

Charlie was only 25 when he died. Along with Eddie Lang, these two were the first in a very long list of guitarists who would die at a tragically young age.

Gibson ES-150 with the Charlie Christian pickup
thanks to Jacques Menach

SILVERTONE GUITARS

That brings us rather neatly to Silvertone. This was a trading name created and owned by Sears Roebuck and was applied to most, if not all, of their electrical, and home entertainment products. The very first item to bear that brand name was a wind-up phonograph which was first offered in 1915. Later on they added a wide range of home radios to their catalogue, amongst other domestic must-haves, which in the fullness of time included televisions. Eventually they moved into the marketing of guitars under the Silvertone brand, replacing the older name of Supertone. However, Sears didn't make these themselves, production was contracted out to avariety of established guitar manufacturers which included Harmony, Kay, Supro, Valco and National (Danelectro being added to the list in latter years as we shall see a little further on). So if you are planning to cruise around the Greater Chicago area looking for the old Silvertone factory you won't find it, as there wasn't one. Their aim was to sell American made, yet affordable, reliable and good quality instruments for use by any player from an amateur to a professional. And they did exactly that.

As early as 1905 Sears had been selling Harmony ukuleles, and in 1916 Sears succeeded in purchasing the Harmony company, although in 1940 the Harmony operation became independent once again. However, Sears continued to retain ownership of the Silvertone name. In the mid 1930s Silvertone brand solid body lap steels first appeared and by 1941 they were offering their first electric Spanish guitars, made to an arch top f-hole format. The first Silvertone solid body electric was launched in 1954, right on the cusp of the rock and roll age, and with perfect timing. Since the '30s the Sears range had included small, by our standards. guitar amplifiers which had been made by the Danelectro company, and in 1954 Danelectro began to make Silvertone guitars too. By the following year the first models withthe now famous lipstick pickups appeared. One of the most memorable Silvertone instruments was the 1457 solid body guitar Amp-In-Case model, much beloved by garage bands everywhere. The case housed the guitar, and also an amplifier and small speaker. Just plug the whole thing into the mains and off you went. Brilliant !!! Didn't really catch on though for some reason. Sears sold off the Silvertone brand in 1972, and it remained moribund for some years until it was purchased by Korean industry giant Samick in 2001. The current Samick Silvertone catalogue features many of those old '60s favourites, all now made in South Korea. It's pleasing to see all of those Harmony and Danelectro style guitars available once more, nostalgia it seems is a major driving force in this industry, and it is also encouraging to see the new generation buying them too. The original ethos of making good quality, reliable, affordable guitars is still very much alive.

1960s Silvertone 319
66409 Archtop
Triple Silver Foil Pickups,
Bigsby
thanks to Tone House

Stratotone Newport
H-42 1955
Metallic Green
thanks to Vintage guitars

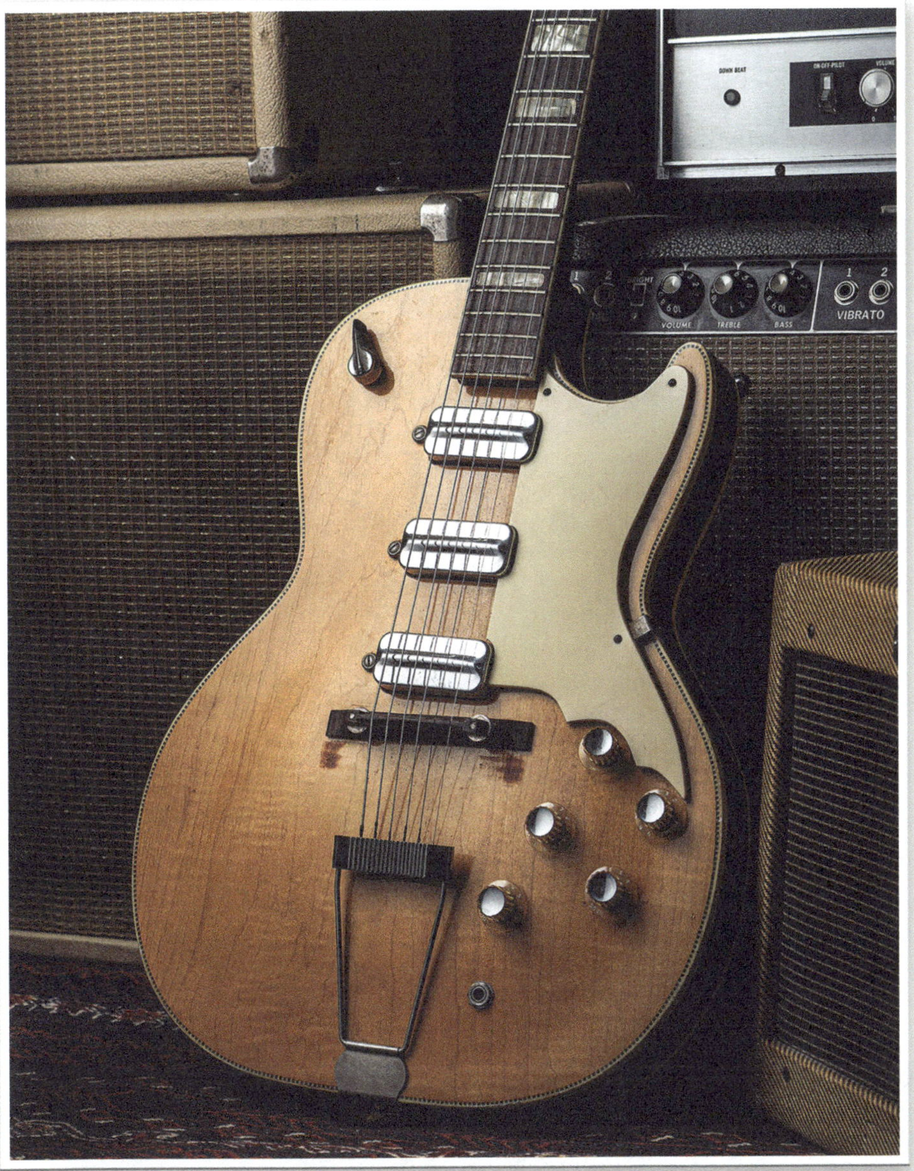

1960
1445 Speed Demon
thanks toJim Hilmar

BERNIE MARSDEN

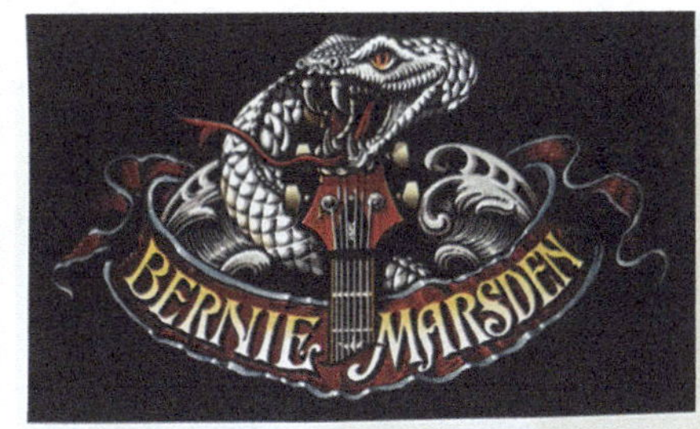

Silvertone - Black - Circa 1960`s

Guitar Service – 25th May 2023

Full Service & Setup including:

Fret polish and fingerboard clean

Clean and lubricate tuners

Checked all electrics

Intonation

Bernie Marsden

Bernie Marsden

The Chris Issak model !

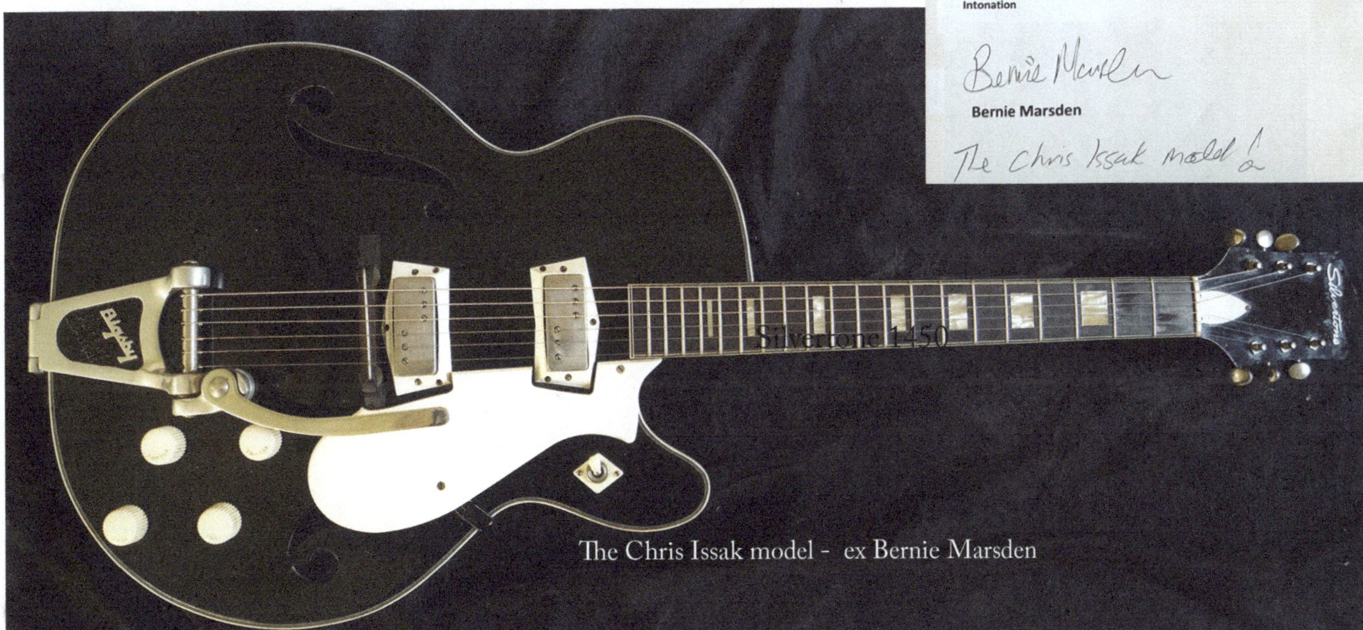

The Chris Issak model - ex Bernie Marsden

LES PAUL - THE LOG

One of the most persistent of tinkerers was guitarist Les Paul, one time sideman to both Nat King Cole and Bing Crosby, and with a string of instrumental hit singles under his belt. He is often referred to as the father of the solid body electric guitar. A pioneer he certainly was, and a brilliant inventor, but the term "father" is pushing it a bit. He had already discovered that an amplified acoustic guitar would howl and feed back if amplified. He'd arrived at the conclusion that a solid body instrument, literally little more than a plank of wood, would not feed back so much, if indeed at all. He cut up an old Epiphone arch top guitar and made a solid body section which basically fitted within it, fitted pickups to it and discovered that he'd solved the problem. The year was 1940. He mooted the idea to the Epiphone company who were not at all interested, and in 1941 he approached Gibson, who also showed no interest in the project. They were far more interested in continuing production of their range of traditional arch top jazz guitars and dismissed the idea of a new fangled solid body. Les had to bide his time until 1950 when Leo Fender's first solid body guitars appeared, and then Gibson's interest was sparked anew. They saw which way the market was headed. Once more Les and Gibson got together, Les explained to them his principles and ideas and left them to come up with a prototype based on those ideas. Essentially what Gibson then did was to shrink down the ES175 body outline, a popular jazz guitar of the time, adapt this into a solid body, and give it a more modern and jazzy finish, hence the metallic painted gold tops. This iconic gold finish was the go-to option for Gibson until 1958 when the sunburst finish Les Paul Standards appeared. These guitars sported the new anti-hum twin coil humbucker pickups designed by Seth Lover a year earlier. These particular guitars are now highly prized and sought after and change hands for significant sums. When Gibson first showed Les the finished prototype guitar he was delighted. As Les Paul was such a major recording artist during the '40s and '50s there was no hesitation whatsoever from either party that it would be called anything other than the Les Paul model, and promoted and marketed as such. In 1952 it was launched to an enthusiastic marketplace. As we all know it was a great success and instantly popular with players from a variety of genres, jazz, rock and roll, country players and so on. The basic design is still very much with us to this day, although the format has been considerably tweaked over the years and there have been a plethora of model variations, all still bearing the Les Paul name, though many of today's younger players have no clue who Les Paul even was. In a sense it has become an industry standard and its timeless ergonomic design will be with us for as long as people still continue to play a guitar.

Les Paul's
Prototype ES-300.

thanks to Lynn Cartwright

In conclusion, from its very humble beginnings in 1928, a mere thirty years later we can readily see how the instrument has come to dominate virtually all genres of popular music. By the late '50s a guitarist could choose from a traditional arch top style jazz guitar, or a slim hollow body design, or a semi solid variation thereof, or a totally solid body instrument, all available in an infinite variety of shapes, finishes, and pickup configurations. There are, by now, also electric 12 strings, 9 strings, twin necks of various types, tenor guitars and so on, and I've barely mentioned bass guitars. The major names and market leaders; Rickenbacker, Gibson, Epiphone, Gretsch, were carry-overs from the prewar era, and postwar continued to establish themselves, expand their ranges, and grow. Others, such as Guild, Fender and Mosrite appeared only after the war, and enthusiastically jumped on the burgeoning bandwagon. Some are gone now, and some names flared only briefly, Messenger for example, founded in 1967 and lasting barely one year. The '50s, it could well be argued, turned out to be the golden age of the electric guitar. Most of us now, and major stars that are much more famous than us mere mortals, regularly play guitars that were first designed 60 or 70 years ago without giving it a second thought. I can't think of any other consumer product of which that could be said. Those classic designs simply don't show their age, that's just because they work so well. You can add or subtract minor features but how can you ever improve on a Telecaster or a Les Paul?

B.B. KING and LUCILLE - live in concert early 1960s

Some pre war jazz players were a bit slow to embrace the new electric guitar. Generally recognized as being the first jazz soloist, Charlie Christian put the guitar on the map, and showed everyone else that it worked. The evolution of the instrument is not therefore due merely to the designers, manufacturers and inventors, but also to the players, who made it visible, and audible. In short order it became a serious instrument instead of a quirky five minute wonder. By the '50s other noted jazz players had followed Charlie's lead, and hence we have legends that have arisen such as Barney Kessel, Johnny Smith, Herb Ellis and Tal Farlow, all of whom had Gibson artist models named after them, as well as other greats such as Kenny Burrell, Sal Salvador and Joe Pass. And not forgetting Les Paul himself of course. Apologies to anyone I failed to name check, but there are so many. Prewar blues singer-guitarists tended traditionally to be soloists, and, in general, didn't play in organized bands. There were hundreds, and I don't intend to list them here, but Robert Johnson is the archetypal prewar blues musician, sat in a chair with his Gibson acoustic of which he is an undeniable master. The electric guitar was made for the blues, and the blues for the electric guitar. One of the first postwar electric blues guitarists to emerge was T Bone Walker, who favoured a full-bodied jazz guitar, as did B B King, until his beloved Lucille, a Gibson ES355 appeared in 1958, an instrument that he used until his death, with just a couple of minor updates. Otis Rush and Buddy Guy both favoured the slim body semi acoustic design, a Epiphone Riviera and Guild Starfire respectively, though they are well known to have used many other guitars during their long careers, though both seem to have been using Fender Stratocasters in later years. Albert King and Albert Collins, both gone now, opted for solid bodies, a Flying V, and a Fender Telecaster respectively. Muddy Waters, one of the earliest high profile blues guitarists, principally played a Telecaster, though he was also rather fond of his Guild Thunderbird.

Many of the early rock and rollers, such as Scotty Moore and Carl Perkins, and slightly later Eddie Cochran and the UK's own Tommy Steele also used full bodied semi acoustics, but when they began their careers the solid bodies had only just been introduced, were still fairly new, and probably viewed with suspicion. The next big name was Chuck Berry who used a slim bodied Gibson ES350 until his Gibson ES345s and ES355s came out in 1958, just like B B King's. During his career he made more records and did more live shows and TV appearances than anyone else I can think of. All of that was beamed via radio and television into American homes on a nightly basis. Everyone wanted to be the next Chuck Berry and he is responsible for selling more guitars than anybody, at least until the Beatles came along anyway. Country players, and come to that Rockabilly players, weren't to be left out, though most of them, Chet Atkins for example, tended to favour Gretsch guitars. They just had "that" sound, not as thick and heavy as the Gibsons, but more mellow and not as bright as the Fenders ,though, as always, there were exceptions. Therefore, apart therefore from stubborn folk fans who wore sandals the electric guitar had caught on in all corners of the musical spectrum, and became the dominant instrument, even supplanting the piano as the most popular. It would be heard in jazz, blues, rock and roll, country, rockabilly and right into mainstream pop, via the instrumental groups and the surfing crazes of the late '50s and early '60s. Even folkies have caught up, especially since Bob Dylan's appearance with a Stratocaster at the 1965 Newport Folk Festival. As we all know this drew a very negative reaction from his fan base. Things inevitably change however, and move on. Many folk groups exist that use electric instruments, and I hope they've finally lost the sandals. That's called progress.

Elmore James was a giant in the history of blues music, and by extension, the electric guitar. He was one who stood astride the transition from traditional Delta Blues, and the raw amplified sound of Chicago Blues, and ultimately its crossover into the mainstream.. He wasn't the only one by any means but, for me, he stands head and shoulders above most of the others due to his 1951 recording of Dust My Broom. That opening slide riff certainly grabs one's attention, and the song became a staple of British blues bands in the '60s, being included in the nightly set lists of every band worthy of the name. As soon as we first heard that raucous sound we all had to copy it without delay. Elmore began his career on a flat top acoustic at a very young age, and it will come as no surprise that Robert Johnson was a significant influence on him and others like J B Hutto and Tampa Red. He also would have learned a lot from his cousin Homesick James, eight years his senior. He took to the electric as if it had been made just for him. He owned many guitars, including a Kay and an Epiphone arch top, and it is said that he liked to play loud. He cut 29 singles during his career, all of which sold in significant quantities. These have become classics in the years since, and justly so, but the seminal Dust My Broom remains his most remembered side, which has been covered countless times. The phrase incidentally is a Mississippi slang term for "I'm going to get out of here". He became referred to as the King Of The Slide Guitar, and laid the foundation for many others who would later absorb and build on his electric technique, such as Ry Cooder, Johnny Winter and Derek Trucks. He died in Chicago in 1963 at the young age of 45. His early death is usually cited as being from a heart attack, but some credible reports say that he was electrocuted by a faulty amplifier. Whatever the cause it was a tragic loss.

THE EARLY ELECTRIC BASS

A bass player is important, and every band or group must have a minimum of one. I am aware that I haven't focused on bass guitars to any great degree so far, but just mentioned a few notable examples in passing, Obviously they do deserve more in depth attention, so here is a potted history of the electric bass guitar. The issues involved in amplifying a standup string bass are unique to that instrument, which after all is fundamentally different to a guitar. Like the guitar, however, people were tinkering and trying to solve the lack of volume problem in the same way. In the early days, prior to the invention of the electromagnetic pickup, piezo transducers were the only way that any acoustic instrument could be amplified. Men like Lloyd Loar, then at Gibson, were toying with such things on basses in the late '20s, but without much success. Following the lead of Rickenbacker's solid body six string designs it was soon accepted that any further attempts to amplify large upright basses were a waste of effort and solid bodies with much smaller dimensions were the way to go. By the mid '30s a number of electric upright basses all appeared at more or less the same time, and establishing which was first across the finish line is virtually impossible. By the middle of the decade there were offerings from Regal, Vega, and Rickenbacker, who'd come up with their solid body Electric Bass Viol, all still upright instruments.

The Rickenbacker featured an arrow shaped aluminum frame a bit like an extended triangle, a jack socket, plus an extending metal stand, and a fairly standard bass neck and fingerboard, so it could be bowed or plucked. In 1935 inventor Paul Tutmarc produced a cello shaped solid body bass that was fretted, and, in theory anyway, could be played upright or horizontally like a guitar, and I surmise that this was the crossover point that defined an upright bass from the first bass guitar deserving of the name. It had been only a matter of time before that simple 90 degree turn had occurred to somebody. The Ampeg Baby Bass, was very similar, but only suitable for upright playing. A very odd Bassoguitar turned up in 1937. Made by Regal it was in essence an oversized round hole flat top guitar, intentionally to be played upright supported by a stand that extended from where an end pin would normally be. Everybody calls these stands pogo-sticks so I will too from here on. It had a fretted fingerboard but the frets were flush with the wood, so acting more as markers than actual frets. All well on the way by now to a purpose built electric bass guitar but we weren't quite there yet. Although bass players in big bands and smaller jazz groups were going some way to solving their volume issue one further problem still existed, and that was one of amplification. Most amps of the time would only deliver around five or six watts, and with those bass frequencies, the speakers sounded like a flatulent cow. Ampeg can be credited with the first dedicated and efficient bass amplifier, and others very soon followed. Following the war development gained momentum.

The first electric bass would come from Paul H Tutmark in Seattle. As chief inventor in the Audiovox company, he would develop a bass guitar from the ideas based on the companies steels and pickups.

Rob Lurvey is shown holding the 1947 Bud Tutmark Electro Bass. Bud was the son of Paul H. Tutmark and these guitars were often mistaken for steel guitars. They were clearly well ahead of the Fender Precision, which would revolutionize the role of the bass in modern music

Harry DeArmond invented the first pickup that could be retrofitted to an acoustic guitar. He produced various different models suitable for both round hole flat tops and archtops. This was in 1935 and a big leap forward. No longer did players have to wait for, or pay extra for, factory made electrics. So successful were his pickups that a wide variety of versions were used by companies such as Harmony, Guild, Gretsch, and others and this continues to this day.

The first Gretsch electric was the Electromatic model that appeared in 1939, still following the then popular trend of an amplified jazz style arch top aimed at the big band players. Many more models would expand the Gretsch catalogue as years passed including solid body instruments. One outstanding, and now much sought after guitar, was the stunning White Falcon, which, at the time of its release, was the most expensive electric guitar ever made.

The advent of World War Two resulted in an inconvenient hiatus in guitar production and any further development. All guitar factories were geared to war production and the making of aircraft components being just one example.

1939 Gretsch Electromatic
Gretsch's first electric guitar, the Electromatic was introduced in 1939. The same year, the Synchromatic archtop guitar series came out. Jimmie Webster, guitar innovator, and player, joins Gretsch.
thanks to Chasingguitars.com

National Electric Spanish Tobacco Sunburst 1935-1938
The National Electric Spanish has a birch top, birch back and sides, chunky V mahogany neck, rosewood fingerboard, Waverly open gear tuners and original large lap steel pickup, This mid 1930s National Electric Spanish guitar is an incredible piece of musical history. Having legitimate claim to be one of the very first electric "Spanish-style" guitars ever made, these guitars are not only rare but represent a crucial transitional period in the history of guitar luthierie. The pickup is large, heavy, and sounds fantastic with a surprisingly big output. It is believed that these pickups are factory-modified lap steel pickups manufactured as part of the National-owned Supro brand.
thanks to Guitar Village (UK) for this submission

1941 Epiphone Electar Spanish Coronet
thanks to Guy Tarium Le Guitarium

Gibson Kalamazoo WWII

An example from the factory where a license was issued allowing children's toys to be built.
Rob Lurvey collection

Scores of writers have written hundreds of books containing millions of words about Gibson guitars. I can add nothing and anything I write here is really superfluous. I'm certainly not going to write words that do no more than repeat everybody else. It is sufficient I feel just to write these few lines. As said elsewhere their first electric, the ES150, appeared in 1936. Gibson swiftly went on to produce electric versions of other full bodied arch top guitars that were already established and popular, such as the L5 and Super 400. The ES175 was launched in 1949, featuring a cheaper laminated top rather than the carved tops used on the L5 etc, available in both single pickup and twin pickup versions. Their first solid, the Les Paul Goldtop, swept onto the market in 1952. As we all know this was followed by many other solid body guitars, the SG's, Firebirds and so on. Thin bodied semi acoustics appeared in 1958, the ES335 and all of its close relatives. Since 1950 Gibson has had four different owners, each of whom have had different ways of doing things and differing ideas regarding what direction the company would take in the years ahead. Out of all of that have come some of the finest guitars ever made, not just by Gibson but by anybody. They've also made some of the worst and I still get cold sweats at the sight of a Corvus, a Dusk Tiger, a Les Paul Professional or Personal, the Eye guitar, and any guitar that features a USB socket. Worst of all however is the truly dreadful Firebird X. What on earth were they thinking? To nobody's great surprise, they didn't sell, and they couldn't even give them away. The only way they could clear inventory was by laying them all out in the Nashville factory car park and running a bulldozer over them.

Before we get ahead of ourselves we should take a close look at the music of the time from 1935 until 1960 when the big bands and jazz musicians were dominating the pop music of the day. The wonderful years of bebop and smooth west coast jazz were taking over and a host of stunning guitarists would emerge. Gibson who were the underdog before WW2 would emerge as the leading company and the sales catalogues would feature the 'All Star' jazz musicians. Epiphone would continue to name models with numerals apart from Al Caiola, leaving the field open to Gibson, who would dominate the market. These were the years of the wonderful artist models, Tal Farlow, Herb Ellis, and Johnny Smith.

Just a few of the remarkable jazz guitarists of this era - they were the guitar heroes long before advent of rock 'n' roll

Gibson Super 400 CES

acoustic models were introduced in 1935 with P90s added and eventually Humbuckers

These were the flagship models and highly desirable with the plectrum guitarists.

thanks to Gary's Classic Guitars

Epiphone Broadway E-251 N Edward Lott

Switchmaster with rare Florentine cutaway

1946 GIBSON ES-300

An arch top guitar, crafted with a mahogany body and featuring an early rounded, no pole piece, P-90. The P-90 pickup was one of the first truly successful single-coil pickups ever developed. The rounded shape of this early model gives it a unique and distinctive sound, with a warmth and clarity that cuts through the mix. Whether you're playing jazz, blues, or rock and roll, this vintage ES delivers a tone that is both classic and timeless.

1952 Gibson ES-175 (left)

Introduced in 1949 the ES-175's all laminate construction meant that costs could be kept down. Initially released with a single neck pickup, it was also the first Kalamazoo design to feature a Florentine cutaway. The ES-175 was only recently discontinued, and is considered one of the greatest jazz guitars. Steve Howe would use the 175 extensively in the rock band Yes. Joe Pass was another jazz player who would create wonderful music on the model With P90s or Humbuckers this is one of Gibson's finest creations.

1957 ES-175 TD (right) the first year in production with PAF Humbuckers.

thanks to ATB Guitars

1958 D'Angelico New Yorker
Recorded in the company ledger as being made in March 1958 and marked on the list as a "Special New Yorker"
Well Strung Guitars

KALAMAZOO GUITARS

The seismic stock market crash happened in 1929. This was immediately followed by the Great Depression which persisted well into the '30s. This era was a disaster for America and its industries, the guitar industry being no exception. Quality American made guitars, such as Gibson, very soon became unfordable for almost everybody. To address this issue and simply just to stay afloat, Gibson launched two new lines of lower priced instruments. These were to be named Kalamazoo and Cromwell. The guitar ranges themselves consisted of round hole flat top acoustics,and f-hole arch tops. They used cheaper tonewoods and cheaper finishes, but at least made reliable and usable American made guitars accessible once more, retailing at a fraction of the price of their Gibson branded big brothers and sisters. The two ranges were broadly similar, and differed only in the way they were marketed. Kalamazoo branded guitars were to be sold principally by mail order giant Montgomery Ward, whereas the Cromwells were sold to wholesale distributors and then on to individual guitar shops around the country, many of whom were already dedicated Gibson dealers. Production of both marques lasted from the early to the late 1930s. By 1939 the nation was pretty much back on its feet so Gibson felt that budget guitars had become redundant, and they didn't wish to undermine sales of the Gibson branded models. In any case, as all of these guitars were acoustic models, they fall outside of the remit of this book. The Kalamazoo brand itself though does not, as it was revived, albeit briefly, in 1966. That year witnessed the introduction of an entry-level solid body guitar bearing the Kalamazoo brand, though "USA" was added to the logo to fend off any potential confusion with Asian imports. The bodies were made of MDF (medium density fibreboard), had a bolt on neck and Melody Maker type pickups. They were available in either red, white or blue and at a glance could easily be mistaken for a Fender Mustang, the outline of which was closely similar. There was one other model which had the shape of an SG, still made from MDF though. This essentially was Gibson's response to the huge influx of cheap Japanese guitars which was in full swing at the time. The experiment was only to last for a year or two, the guitars were fairly horrible and weren't well received at the time. Just ten years later the company decided instead to use a different strategy when they demoted Epiphone to be their budget label and moved all production to the Far East where it continues to this day.

1942-Kalamazoo-KG32 Heritage Auctions

1939 Kalamazoo KETG 14
4 string with added pickup
Rob Lurvey collection

KG-2A in Dakota Red
Chicago Guitar Exchange

KG-1 in Sonic Blue
Chicago Guitar Exchange

1966 KG2 Wunjo Guitars

A short history of the electric guitar pickup

At the risk of stating the obvious the most essential components of any electric guitar are the pickups. Without them a guitar would be like a bird without wings, suitable only for propping open the garden shed door, or to be converted into a stylish wall clock. The sound and tonal signature of any guitar is due to its many components, the body, the wood that the body happens to be made from, the way it is put together, and all of the other hardware, but the heart and soul of it all are the pickups.

Since the very earliest days of the electric guitar a lot of research, and trial and error, has been expended on the best way of coming up with a practical version of this vital part. Some experiments were more successful than others and have become standard equipment, others less so. Like the Stromberg Electro the first amplified guitars used a variety of transducers or contact microphones. None of these things were entirely satisfactory and something designed specifically for guitars and other stringed instruments was sought. The answer was the electromagnetic pickup, first seen on the Rickenbacker Frying Pan. This was the invention, as said elsewhere, of George Beauchamp. All other manufacturers quickly came up with their own interpretations of this device, and although varying slightly in the way they were designed, the basic scientific principle remained constant.

All early pickups consisted of just one coil. One unavoidable side effect of this was an annoying 50 cycle hum (60 cycles in the US). This was induced in any pickup from unshielded mains voltage. This could come from anywhere, even if you got too close to your own amplifier, but was especially prevalent under stage lighting or fluorescent tubes. This issue wasn't to be solved until Seth Lover came up with his hum-bucker unit. More on that later. Incidentally that 50 cycle per second, or hertz, hum, can be a useful guitar tuner. A bottom octave G is 49 hertz, and Ab is 51.4. Get your lowest G somewhere in there, accounting for the correct octave of course, and you're pretty much there.

Charlie Christian pickup

The first commercial electric guitar pickup with the Gibson ES-150 and the start of the electric guitar revolution

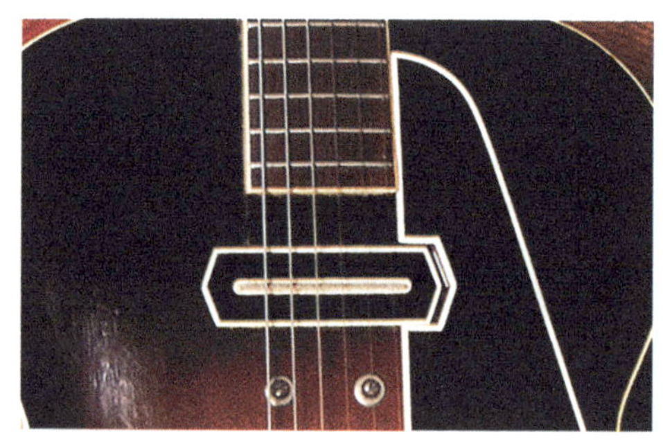

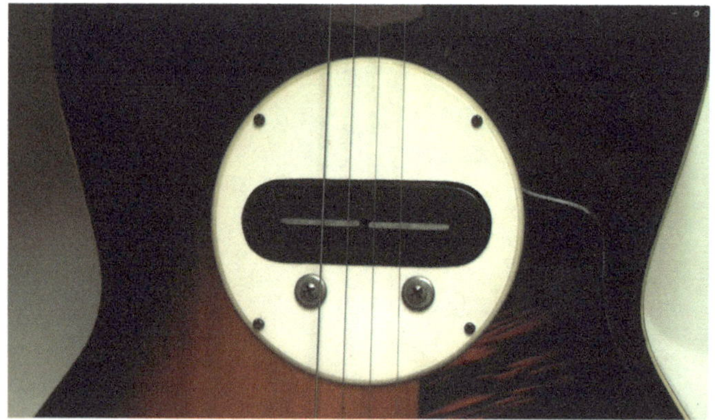

KETG 14 Kalamazoo Electric Tenor 4 string Guitar

Kalamazoo was the Gibson budget brand. The sound hole is filled with plastic and the pickup set inside

1939 Rickenbacker made from bakelite

Fitted with pickup and vibrola which was made from sewing machine parts. They made approx 44 of these instruments

The Rob Lurvey Collection

y early Rick with a solid wood bo
rototype or a very limited produc

During the early thirties, the Electric Spanish style guitar finally took off after the late twenties acoustically amplified resophonic National and Dobros. With many of the same people involved, it naturally continued with Adolph Rickenbacker, Paul Barth, George Beauchamp creating the electromagnetic guitar pickup based on the phonograph cartridge needle and telephone diaphragm ideas. The RoPatIn Elektro A-25 Frying Pan soon took off with Alvin McBurney Alvino Rey and Sol Hoopii playing popular Hawaiian steel guitar.

Here are a few of the earliest versions built. Regal in Chicago made these small bodies for Rickenbacker, Dobro and National. One of the very earliest shipped models shown here is in North Dakota in a prestigious museum. The third one pictured in black & white has a white ceramic coated horseshoe magnet pickup with a lightly sunbursted smaller body. It was at my second vintage guitar show we did at SIR Hollywood studios in 1980 and photographed by fellow guitar historian Tom Wheeler for his American Guitars book. Tom was later an editor with Guitar Player magazine and recently passed. It was owned for years by a friend who worked for Rickenbacker and custom builds great versions to customers specs. He can't remember who bought it unfortunately. I am actively looking for this very instrument.
thanks to Robb Lawrence for these photos and information

The Beauchamp/Barth horseshoe pickup by Paul Brett

It's a long story and very contentious over who exactly started the whole thing off, many contenders were arriving at a very similar solution around the same period. Overall it is generally accepted that the horseshoe pickup, designed in 1931 (patented in 1937) by George Beauchamp and put into a wooden prototype body built by British Royal Navy veteran, HarryWatson, creating the Rickenbacker Frying Pan which became the first commercially viable and available electric guitar. But exactly where did Beauchamp create his pickup? Well, it didn't happen overnight, and he didn't do it on his own. George had been working with Paul Barth for many years at the National company, right from the days of the creation of the resonator with the Dopyera brothers. George and Paul had a strong professional and personal connection, they became great buddies. George, a popular musician was heavily involved in the entertainment and party scene of the day. Paul would join George and flying ace, racing driver Eddie Rickenbacker (cousin of Adolph) at social events and parties across Los Angeles. Embarrassingly, for Eddie, a professional driver, once crashing their car into a tree!

Since Beauchamp was chasing the dream of an electric/amplified guitar he and Paul Barth, collaborated over many months, not only at George's home but also at Paul Barth's parents' home. (Barth's daughter Sharon Sagar confirms this, Nolan Beauchamp talked about it and also guitar historian Robb Lawrence) Paul's parents were Martin Barth and Irma (Dopyera). Paul's brother Carl was also living at the house. It is known that Beauchamp and Barth were using motors from a washing machine and also Irma's sewing machine. Paul Barth's daughter, Sharon Sagar, recalls, "Beauchamp and her Dad (Paul) were working on Irma's kitchen table, and were playing around with electricity, which then caused a blackout in LA!!! That is why they got in trouble with Irma! Eventually, George and Paul found the right configuration and finally they had a working design for the horseshoe pickup and created the first commercially viable electric guitar. Harry Watson created the body and Adolph Rickenbacker backed the new invention. George being very astute commercially and in business raised the patent (eventually) and took credit for the design. Paul, being more technical but less commercially aware, also raised a patent for a detachable horseshoe pickup. So, where exactly was the Rickenbacker Model A-22 Electro Hawaiian lap steel guitar, nicknamed the 'frying pan' created? At George Beauchamp's home, and on Irma Barth's kitchen table and all combined at the National String Instrument Corp factory to make the final product.

A short history of the electric guitar pickup - The Humbucking background

The principle of hum-cancelling was first used in Ampex Tape recorder machines and developed for very early pickups in the late 1930s. Gibson and Gretsch were looking to find a solution to the hum levels produced when incurring higher volumes. Seth Lover and Ray Butts were the two key figures in the conception of what would prove to be one of the most exciting inventions in the history of the electric guitar.

As I touched upon earlier the universally popular humbucker pickup was designed by Seth Lover (pronounced Low-ver). A native of Kalamazoo and having a wealth of experience in electronics gained principally from his years of military service. It was almost an inevitability that he would wind up working for Gibson. His early time there was taken up by the designing and building of Gibson's amplifiers and it wasn't long before he became aware of the 60 cycle hum conundrum. His solution was to have a pickup made up of two coils, one fitted in the opposite polarity to the other, effectively putting them out of phase. This, he was relieved to discover, almost entirely eliminated hum. It further transpired that the tone they produced was something different, very good bottom end response, better sustain, a higher output, and overall, a sound best described as being more meaty. The copper wire was wound into coils individually of course and the bobbin the coil was formed around was attached to the spindle of an electric motor. It was then sent spinning and the operator would cease the process when, in his opinion, the coil appeared to be full. He wouldn't even have had a number counter in those early days so I leave you to imagine the variations in pickup performance that resulted. Lover invented this pickup in 1955, beating Gretsch's own humbucker design by two years, but his patent application was not passed until 1959. The pickups made between those years are known as Patent Applied For pickups, or PAF's for short. They have small black and gold decals on the mounting plates. They are highly desired and easily fetch four figure sums on the collectors market. They were not fitted to a production model guitar until 1957 when a pair were fitted to an ES175, the first guitar to carry them. Soon after the then popular Les Paul Goldtop guitar gained two and morphed into the Les Paul Standard, and in the same year a Les Paul Custom was launched which sported three. Other models also inherited humbuckers as a standard component, such as the Byrdland, ES5 Switchmaster and, ES350. Entire ranges of new Gibson models appeared in 1958, including the Flying V and Explorer, plus the ES335, 345 and 355. All were equipped with Seth Lover 's humbuckers. Those now classic Les Paul guitars, and the humbucker pickups, are still in production. They have become the standard by which all other pickups are judged.

The best known of the independent pickup manufacturers were DeArmond, who began back in 1939, when Harry DeArmond first offered his add-on pickups. The company rightfully grew in reputation, so when the Guild Guitar Company was founded in 1952 and who immediately began producing a spectacular range of full bodied semi acoustic jazz style guitars, DeArmond pickups throughout the range were the only logical way to go. Guitars made by Kay, Harmony and others, even including those under the Silvertone brand, fitted DeArmond's pickups exclusively. Those famous Harmony Gold Foil pickups were DeArmonds and as Harmony claimed to be the largest guitar makers in the world back then they must have bought literally millions of them.

Thomas V Jones was guitar repairer and occasional luthier who had a fascination (obsession?) for recreating the original sound of Gretsch Filtertron pickups. This fascination was largely driven by one of his best customers, a certain Brian Setzer. In 1993 he finally launched a line of such items, intended to replace original fittings, or those found on the Gretsch guitars which by then were largely being made in China. He offered eight different versions. The one that appealed most to me was the Thunder-tron. That's just got to be good. T V Jones pickups have also been factory fitted to non Gretsch guitars including a couple of editions of a Fender Telecaster. In 2008 Jones introduced a line of guitars, made in the Japanese Terada facility, grandly entitled the Spectra Sonic Supreme model, which bears the T V Jones logo on the headstock. All of these, although a variety of finishes and additional components are available, carry the same Jones pickups. The body is a classic single cutaway pattern and is chambered for weight relief. These are a craftsman made instrument produced to high standards in one of Japan's very longest lived and most respected makers and are a long way indeed from being a cheap copy.

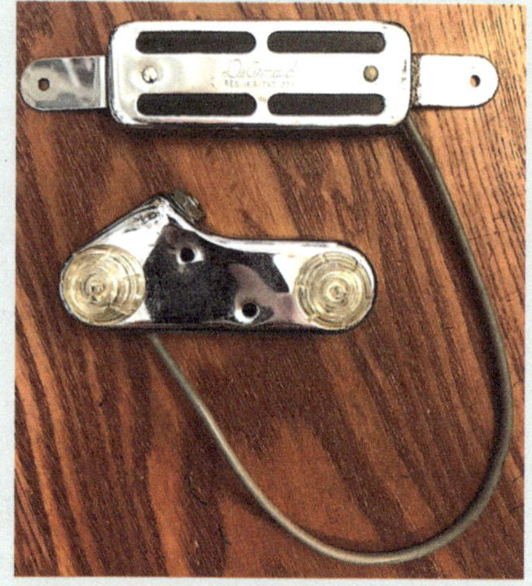

1955 ES-350 TD

Perhaps the first Gibson to be fitted with humbuckers below is an extract of conversation between Seth Lover and Seymour Duncan

thanks to Neil Flemming (UK)

What were the first instruments if you can recall that the humbucker was used on? Would it be the solid body or acoustic?

As I recall, I could be wrong, but I think it was the ES-350. It was not the thin one. It was the full sized body, as I recall, and then shortly after we put it on the Les Paul solid body. They still had the other early style, I guess, the ES-[illegible]25 with the cream cover (dog ear P-90) that was fit down [illegible] the body. And they had that on some because people liked that particular style of pickup. And then we added – the ES-335 – that was a thin model.

How did you figure out the distance between the pickup and the bridge, not making it too close or too far away?

That was pretty much trial and error. You used what was basically used before as the position. And you might have tried it a little forward or a little backwards to see if you could get any particular improvement, but I thing that it was pretty well mind set by a musician as to the position. They liked to have certain – they thought was correct for the pickup. And if you started fighting a musician by moving it to some place he didn't like you could get into trouble. Now if you came back too close to the bridge you could get it a little brighter, but you had a tendency to lose volume because the string vibration d[illegible] [illegible]ove[illegible] [illegible]f you lost too much volume because the[illegible] [illegible]were [illegible] dog-house because you were not as lo[illegible] therefore, [illegible] were not as good.

A short history of the electric guitar pickup

Any of us now can choose from an overflowing shop display cabinet of pickups which might well include not merely the long established DiMarzio brand, but also those made by Kent Armstrong, EMG, Seymour Duncan, Bartolini, Mighty Mite, Bare Knuckle, Bill Lawrence, Lindy Fralin, Amalfitano and others. Just to muddy the waters still further both Fender and Gibson also market their own full ranges of replacements and upgrades often reproductions of their classic originals. That's a lot of pickups to choose from. You can find replacement units for any guitar, from a Danelectro to a Gibson P90, or Firebird and any variety of humbucker or single coil Fender style unit. At time of writing the market leaders are certain to be DiMarzio with around 200 pickups in their current catalogue.

In the early '50s, Leo Fender had joined the fray putting his own unique stamp on things. By the 1970s companies emerged who were making just pickups, the intention was that they could be retrofitted quickly and easily to any guitar, at the same time claiming that they were more efficient than factory stock units. A prime example would have to be the output of Larry DiMarzio who began to design, build and sell pickups in 1971, including the near legendary Super Distortion humbucker. They were designed with just one purpose in mind, and that was more power! Scores of other pickup manufacturers have cropped up in the years since, all with the common goal of producing drop-in units which promise to dramatically improve the tone and/or volume of an existing guitar. When I was working in the shop during the '70s I was, on a daily basis, confronted by a steady stream of players who wanted their guitars supercharged. It didn't seem to matter what it was, "Just Rip Those Out And Stick Some DiMarzio's In It" was the plaintive cry, which usually concluded with "I'll be back in a half hour". It would have been totally understandable if they'd been bringing in a cheap Japanese copy, but they invariably were placing Gibsons or Fenders on the counter. Now, fifty years on, people are having to spend lots of money to restore those same guitars to their original spec.

Old pickups versus New and the vintage market

There is no doubt the tone of vintage pickups have that magic quality which is so desired by major players and collectors. There is a distinct warmth to the sound, especially the high E and B strings which is more pleasing to the ear than new guitars which can sound harsh and metallic. In the hands of the right person a Gibson Les Paul Burst will come to life especially when being driven hard The word 'growl and bark' are used to describe the unique sound of these old pickups. Many years ago when speaking to Jeff Beck's tech. I asked the usual question "How does he get that great tone?" I was surprised when he was quite open, describing some of the techniques they employed with one feature being - Jeff would resort to stripping down a '50s Strat which was past its best just to get at the all important magnets which would then be re-built. The theory was that the old magnets were the Alnico type and included the essential Cobalt which added to the impurities in the slugs.

Old wive's tales and theories, who knows! but there is the undeniable fact that modern pickups do lack that organic warmth.

Truss Rods

I'd like to write a few words about truss rods. This might initially sound a little dull but the subject is an important one, and has a lot to do with the evolution of the guitar, any guitar at that, not just electrics. Back in the olden days guitars had gut strings which didn't exert much tension on the necks and bodies of guitars. When steel guitar strings became commonly available around 1900 or so guitar necks, which are obviously only made of wood, were expected to handle the higher tension strings, but instead started to pull upwards creating a concave bow in the neck, and a very high action, much to the dismay of guitar players everywhere. This problem needed to be addressed and as usual tinkerers began to work on solutions to the issue. As early as 1908 patents were being applied for which proscribed several variations of a basic steel rod which could be inserted into the neck thus preventing the neck bending in this way. Gibson addressed the issue in a different way by inserting a V shaped length of rock maple along the neck under the fretboard, and Martin did something very similar but with a square section length of ebony. The sheer hardness and non flexibility of these woods would, it was hoped, prevent neck warpage. What was needed though was a method of adjusting the neck to suit different playing styles. A medium-ish set of guitar strings will exert a tension of around 150 to 160 pounds, and that is constantly pulling the strings between the headstock and the bridge. Just try lifting a tank with 15 gallons of water in it and you will get some notion of the forces that the structure of a guitar has to contend with. That string tension would be increased by a further 30% or so on a twelve string guitar. Even a light gauge set still has a tension of about 120 pounds. What was required was an adjustable rod that could be made to compensate for that force by pulling the neck in the opposite direction and even it out. It wasn't just a simple matter of string gauge either. Some blues players, and country players, used various different tunings, each one subtly altering the overall string tension. Wood necks were also sensitive to climatic changes, even changes in humidity or ambient temperature.

The fact of the matter was, and at the risk of labouring the point, that wood bends, and thus a neck needs regular adjustment. It was a Gibson employee named Thaddeus McHugh who came up with the solution and in 1921 he obtained a patent for such a device. It was a major leap forward in guitar construction, and playability. It consisted of a steel rod set into a groove in the neck, mounted directly beneath the fretboard, threaded at both ends, a brass nut at the headstock end, a fixed nut at the heel end to prevent the whole thing becoming unscrewed and falling out, and the rod itself passing through a captive steel plate at each end. Although different makers might have used slightly different designs or hardware the principle throughout remained the same. Adjustment would be easily done by means of a hexagonal wrench, sometimes an Allen key or even a screwdriver depending on the make. So regardless of string gauge, the tuning, or even the weather one could at last have a guitar with a straight neck. Today all guitars have them with the exception of those with aluminum necks which are so rigid any adjustable truss rod would be superfluous.

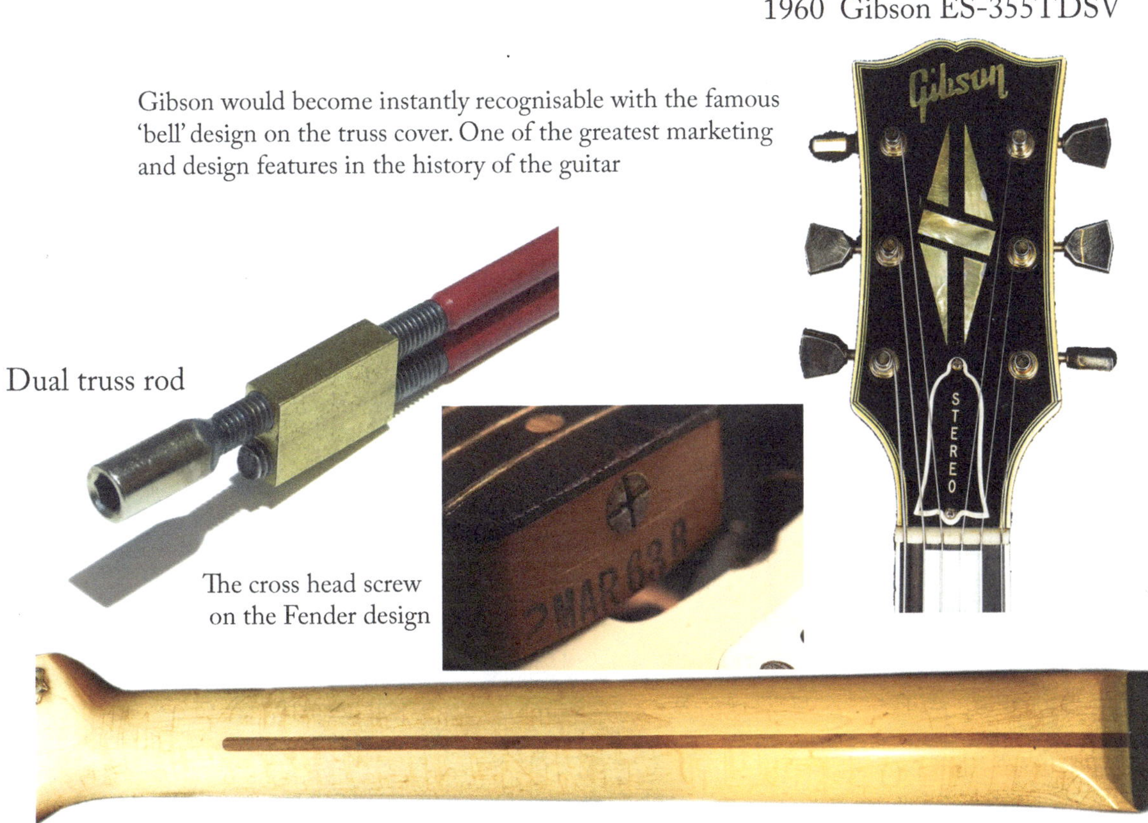

1960 Gibson ES-355TDSV

Gibson would become instantly recognisable with the famous 'bell' design on the truss cover. One of the greatest marketing and design features in the history of the guitar

Dual truss rod

The cross head screw on the Fender design

HARMONY GUITARS

Harmony

SINCE 1892

One name that has bubbled to the surface several times throughout this book is that of Harmony especially concerning their early involvement with building Rickenbacker bodies, the many years of Silvertone production, and the location of their current home at the old Gibson plant in Kalamazoo. The long history of the Harmony company extends right back to the final decade of the 19th century. As our focus is firmly on electric guitars and their specific story the earliest years of the Harmony company's existence don't directly concern us here so I'm not getting into that area. If you really need the full story there are many sources for you to delve into. So we are going to skip a decade or two. As has previously been mentioned the Chicago based Harmony company was bought by Sears Roebuck in 1916. At this time they manufactured ukuleles, mandolins, violins, banjos, and guitars, the quantities of which increased as guitars became more popular with blues musicians and guitarists in jazz bands of various types. By 1923 Sears were selling 250.000 Harmony brand instruments annually, making it easily the largest guitar company in the world. By 1930 that number had doubled. More was to come as by 1965 in the wake of the British Invasion when simply everybody had to have a guitar and annual sales had topped 350.000. It has been said that between 1945 and 1975 a grand total of ten million Harmony guitars were sold, so it's a fair bet that all of us will have owned one at some point. The very first Harmony electric, an f-hole arch top guitar seems to have appeared around 1937 or 1938, though definitive details are a bit sketchy and the first electric solids in 1954. In the years since many model varieties have been catalogued, from solid bodies like the Bobcat and Comet basses, and those well known semi acoustics like the Rocket, Stratotone, H75's through H78's, and the H79 12 string. Even the relatively low priced Harmony guitars were unable to combat the Japanese tide and the company went belly-up in 1975.

From being the largest in the world to insolvency in a generation must have been a bitter pill to swallow. Restitution arrived in 2018 when the marque was purchased by Singapore based BandLab Technologies. Thus it is Harmony guitars are once again being made in the USA and also reproductions of many of those much missed classic models are being produced under the Samick banner in South Korea. Before I leave this subject I must pass on my favourite quote. It was said by the then boss of Harmony back in the '60s, and is, "We might make a million guitars, but we only make them one at a time".

1967 Harmony H27, Sunburst Andy Baxter

Harmony H617 Bobkat Luthiery Laboratories

KAY GUITARS

Just recently I was perusing historic photos of blues musicians, scores of them, taking special note of those playing electric guitars. During the '30s and '40s, and right through to the '50s, many of those photos showed blues guitarists playing electric instruments predominantly from Kay, Harmony, and Silvertone. Those were tough times, still in the throes of the depression, there was little money around, and few could afford those desirable Gibsons and Epiphones. Kay, Harmony, and a couple of other makes such as Vega, supplied affordable budget priced, yet acceptable quality instruments and gave those guys the stepping stones to better things, as without those guitars many of those players would never have gone on to the next step and we never would have heard them at all. Hence their importance should not be underestimated or ignored. Most of those early performers cut their teeth in cities like New Orleans, and in bars and juke joints across the south. The great migration to the industrial cities in the north, particularly Chicago, carried on throughout those decades. and took the blues along with it. The mean and unwelcoming streets of Chicago transformed the music forever, and it became raw and louder. A different style was born, the Chicago blues and the electric guitar was an integral part of that. Many of those singers and guitar players ended up on the sidewalks of Chicago's Maxwell Street, running a mains cord into the nearest shop so they could be heard as they almost all had amplifiers by this time. Many legendary names emerged from that scene, especially from the Southside, and the West Side.. Names like Muddy Waters and Howlin' Wolf, far too many to mention here. We all know what happened. As Muddy said, "The blues had a baby and they called it rock and roll". The Maxwell Street scene gradually ebbed away, the local club scene grew and became the highly organized and successful enterprise that it is now. Even, though I hesitate to mention it, a must on the tourist trail. I cannot emphasize enough the importance of the relationship between the electric guitar and the blues, and all of the seminal rock music that it gave life to in later years. One feeds the other, and without that symbiosis, we would have neither, and we'd all be playing the accordion. Anyway, I seem to have wandered off the point of this. which is the guitars themselves, so I will turn my attention to that very subject. Kay was founded in 1931, by a man named Henry 'Kay' Kuhrmeyer, and he had history, having previously worked for Andrew Groehsl's company, who had been making a variety of stringed instruments since as far back as 1890. During the '20's the firm owned Stromberg who produced, as mentioned earlier, the very first electric guitar, which is why you are reading this book. Kay made their first electric, a slim-bodied semi-acoustic, in 1936, the same year as Gibson's ES150 arrived. In 1937 they produced a three quarter size upright electric bass. For the remainder of the decade, into the '40s, '50s and beyond they focused on producing a wide range of affordable electric guitars, often referred to now as 'blue collar' guitars, which says it all.

How many Kay, Silvertone guitars etc can you see in the wonderful collection of Rob Lurvey. Botton left shows a great flamey Kay from 1939 in pristine condition

A particularly popular model was the Thin Twin K-161, first appearing in 1950 and seen in the hands of Jimmy Reed, and Chuck Berry before he became famous. Their wide range featured full-bodied arch top guitars, thin semis, solids, and regular flat top acoustics, and always at friendly prices, but of professional quality. In 1957 they came up with a Barney Kessel signature model, which remained in the catalogue until 1962. For the UK market they produced another signature model for British blues pioneer Alexis Korner. Kay also manufactured a wide range of budget priced guitars bearing other brand names, Kent being one example, the bulk of which were made specifically for retailers such as Montgomery Ward, Sears Roebuck and J C Penney. In 1952 the K-162 electric bass guitar appeared, the big brother of the K-161. Other popular models were the Red Devil, a double cutaway semi, and the Speed Demon, a single cutaway model that came in one, two, or three pickup variations, and it was one of these that became Eric Clapton's first 'proper' guitar.

Most other British guitarists would have started their careers on one of those too. Just being 'cheap' however wasn't enough for Kay, and they moved upmarket with their Gold Line series, which were handmade to much higher standards and specifications. This range was in production from 1957 until 1962 and it has to be said was not a great success. Hard times were ahead for Kay in a steadily more overcrowded market, especially when competing against the Japanese invasion of hyper cheap guitars, and the company was sold to jukebox manufacturers Seeburg in 1965. Two years later the company was sold to Valco. In 1969 the company was sold again, but has had so many other owners since that quite frankly I've lost track. I do know that the Kay name has somehow survived and budget priced guitars are currently being made under the brand, though this time in Asia.

GRIMSHAW GUITARS

Grimshaw

"ELECTRACOUSTIC" GUITARS

Although by the outbreak of the Second World War, most American guitar makers already had electric guitars of one type or another in full production, over in the UK things were a little slower getting into gear, a fact I alluded to a few pages ago. The very first UK made electric guitar was the Premiervox of 1935, a lap steel guitar assembled by Emile Grimshaw and Company from parts imported from Rickenbacker. The first Spanish style electric was another Grimshaw, the Plectric, (clever) a single pickup arch top introduced in 1948. From that point onwards Grimshaw introduced many other electrics, including solid bodies, one of which was the very successful GS-30, a cheeky copy of Gibson's Les Paul Standard. These were made from 1968 until 1971 and were a viable alternative to the Gibson original, which, in any case, was itself out of production at this time. One of these was much used by Status Quo guitarist Francis Rossi. Grimshaw made a range of other electrics as the years passed, both jazz guitars and solids. which included 12 strings and twin necks. Grimshaw did not own a very large factory, hence production totals remained stubbornly low, and largely for that reason they never really entered the mainstream. In the seventies, and in common with many other makers, they found themselves unable to compete with cheaper Japanese imports, and the company finally ceased trading in 1985.

This is an illustration of one of the models in Grimshaw's Plectric series."

RICKENBACKER GUITARS

Adolph Rickenbacker George Beauchamp

Rickenbacker's early inventions and forays into electric guitar production have been reviewed earlier in this volume, and vital they undeniably were. There are gaps in the story however, and I will use this space to fill in some blanks, and expand on the overall tale. The company was founded by Adolph Rickenbacher, the name later Americanized to Rickenbacker. He was born in Basel Switzerland in 1886, and came to America with his family in 1891, at which time he would have been five years old. They originally settled in the Midwest but Adolph later relocated to Southern California. Adolph's father, also Adolph, a pattern maker, died in Columbus Ohio in 1939. Adolph Jr was a mechanical engineer and, with the help of his family's finances, opened up a tool and die factory. As luck would have it he wound up owning the only deep-draw sheet steel press in the region, and his factory was soon contracted to manufacture the bodies for National steel resonator guitars, and a number of other components too. He became friendly over time with Paul Barth and George Beauchamp, both of whom were then working on developing a practical electrified guitar, and in 1931 they formed a company which they named RoPatin. It was in that year that their first joint venture, the legendary Frying Pan appeared. As described earlier, this was very successful and between 1931 and 1939, 2700 examples were made. The company continued evolving their ranges of both guitars and amplifiers and by the outbreak of the war had become firmly established. Adolph served in both World Wars, but by 1946 he appears to have lost interest in the guitar industry, which, being principally an engineer by trade, he'd never been especially interested in anyway. The company seems to have been slowly wound down, and guitar production tailed off. Enter Francis C Hall. He was a financier and entrepreneur with a special interest in the musical industry. He owned a firm, named the Radio And Television Equipment Company, and In 1948 he joined forces with Leo Fender. The nationwide promotion and distribution of Fender products were Hall's job, whilst Leo, who had little interest in such trivialities, concentrated on making guitars and amplifiers. Many stories abound that Leo and Francis didn't get along and there existed an ongoing clash of personalities. I have to interject here to say that when I was working for the UK Rickenbacker importers and distributors in the '70s we found that Mr Hall wasn't the easiest person to deal with. For example, we might order ten 4001 basses, but he'd only send two, and make us feel grateful that we'd even got those. However, I digress. In 1953 Hall saw an opportunity to purchase Rickenbacker and consequently, he and Leo parted ways. For Rickenbacker, this was a watershed moment. Old Rickenbacker had become New Rickenbacker, and it was Hall who invigorated the company and piloted it to its next phase. He immediately set about designing totally new ranges of solid body electrics having absorbed some of the know-how from Leo Fender. These would still feature Barth's and Beauchamps's pickups, and in this same year, Roger Rossmeisl had joined the company. Rossmeisl was a jazz guitarist and skilled luthier recently migrated from post war Germany. He had already served a short stint it the Gibson factory in Kalamazoo before deciding to head west where he threw in his lot with Rickenbacker. Some of the early guitars were quite bizarre and not very appealing or saleable, but in 1956 the first notable guitars, the Combo 400 series, appeared. Just a single pickup version initially, but twin pickup versions appeared two years later. Also in 1958, the first semi solid guitars were launched. This was the Capri, which eventually evolved into the 300 range of guitars that are with us today, all designed by Rossmeisl, with a certain Semie Moseley as his apprentice. Rossmeisl stayed at Rickenbacker until 1962 when he was to join Fender. Some oddballs have appeared in the intervening years, including the Eddie Peabody Banjoline, (shown right) a sort of guitar/banjo mash up, the Eddie Peabody Bantar, which had a conventional banjo shape but with a solid body, and also the 331LS, pictured on the following page, which incorporated an internal light show. Francis Hall retired in 1984 and passed the torch to his son John, who continues the tradition, moving the company along to keep pace with changing tastes, and introducing new models, or upgrading older ones. Those classic original outlines though still remain. The company proudly assures us that all guitars are made exclusively in the Santa Ana factory. They don't make anything offshore, and have a zero tolerance approach when it comes to copies, whether they come from Asia or anywhere else. Francis C Hall passed away in 1999. Adolph Rickenbacker died in 1976, just a couple of weeks short of his 90th birthday. He is interred in Loma-Vista Memorial Park in Fullerton. His headstone carries the inscription "Father Of The Electric Guitar".

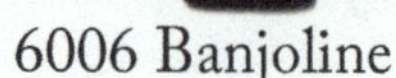

6006 Banjoline

331LS model with the internal light show

1968 366/12
1987 360/12 in tuxedo colors
Craig Brody

thanks to John Shannon

Rickenbacker 360F Capri original. This guitar is one of just sixteen Mapleglo finish 360F models made in 1960, and one of forty Mapleglo models made overall in this guise according to Rickenbacker factory invoices.

LEO FENDER

I'm sure we are all familiar with the story of Leo Fender or should be, so I'm not going to reprise all of that here. Suffice it to say that Leo, although not a guitarist himself but a radio repairer and electronics wizard, had found himself making guitar amplifiers, primarily for lap steel guitarists. Once the war was over he came up with the notion of building some lap steels himself, and fitting them with his own hand wound pickups, an area that held a particular fascination for him. His first solid body lap steels were allegedly made in 1945 following the end of the Second World War, though some sources cite "the early '40s" for the earliest examples, so a definitive date remains unclear. They were, however, well received, particularly in the genre known as Western Swing, and as a result of positive comments, he decided to experiment with a solid bodied conventional Spanish guitar. He started work on what were to become the Esquire and Broadcaster (later Telecaster) models in 1948, and after some trial and error, and more tweaking, those guitars were launched in 1950. Although not entirely accurate many people view these as being the first real electric guitars and revere them as such. They were certainly simple, and crucially, cheap and quick to manufacture. Just a slab of wood with a screwed on neck and a pickup or two. The design became iconic and has never dated, and Fender continues to manufacture thousands of these yearly. As a guitar it works perfectly and every player will have one at some point in his or her career, and rightly so. Leo went on to produce a wealth of other Fender models, the Jazzmaster, Jaguar, Mustang, the entry level Bronco and so on, including the Precision Bass, the first bass guitar, but his most iconic, and universally popular model, was the Stratocaster, launched in 1954. In sheer numbers, this is arguably the most popular guitar ever, the Volkswagen Beetle of the guitar world. The design is a work of genius and still looks as modern now as it did over 70 years ago. Every player, famous or not, will be playing a Stratocaster somewhere along the line.

1954 #0504
1955 # 09635
thanks to Yoshi Aono

Fender Jazz Bass
1965 Shoreline Gold
Well Strung Guitars

1950 Broadcaster
0207
Francesco Balossino (C'èsco s Corner)

FENDER

Probably the most popular guitars on the planet, their designs copied by many but never surpassed. A Fender guitar can be adapted to suit the style of any player and equipped with controls and a pickup selector switch laid out in an ergonomic fashion making the instruments easy to use and virtually idiot proof. Many guitarists would eventually turn to Fender and create their own unique sound. Much has been written about the Stratocaster, however, 1954 to 1965 were the finest years and guitarists usually have their favourite year. The normal finish for this era was sunburst but there were exceptions such as the Mary Kaye model (known as "The First Lady of Rock and Roll" and the first endorsee). 1956 would also see some blonde finishes or special factory ordered colours. From '59 the rosewood neck was introduced, and a body choice of sunburst or custom colour taken from the DuPont car range, (Burgundy Mist, Sonic Blue, Olympic White etc), there was quite a list. The sound changed to a warmer tone and the guitars featured on so many great recordings. After 1965 quite a few of the guitars still used the pre-CBS parts and are still in demand from vintage enthusiasts. In the late '60s Jimi Hendrix would explode into the music world and create a whole new fan base of the model. New design features were introduced in the '70s, and some say the model lost some of the magic. The three bolt neck plates were certainly innovative and neck pitch adjustment more convenient. Artists such as Pete Townshend and Ritchie Blackmore would favour this era and create some of rock's defining sounds. The Jaguars, Jazzmasters and Telecasters found popularity with all genres including, country, surf, rockabilly and rock bands. The Precision and Jazz basses took the music world by storm with their never before heard tonal clarity.

thanks to Jacques Menache

thanks to Crai Brody

1954 Stratocaster
0663 with rare figured/flame neck
Francesco Balossino (C'èsco s Corner)

GIBSON 1950 - 1970

The 1950s would see the extraordinary years of Gibson competing with Fender, but in their own way with craftsmen built instruments incorporating the advances in electronics. The Goldtops changed over the decade morphing into the Burst years of 1958 1960. The Sunburst was aimed at the jazz player and largely ignored until the UK rock and blues players discovered the magical quality of the overdriven sound. Eric Clapton after listening to Freddie King gave us the wonderful Beano LP and the sound which is still being copied. Much has been written about this period of the Gibson company and we are content to leave the reader with some great examples from that era which would see some great ES and SG models coming out from the Gibson factory

9 1923 Donna The story of the Bursts is well documented elsewhere but this 1959 is a superb example. The Bursts are the top of the tree for collect-ability and prices remain at an all time high. Truly wonderful sounding guitars and they have played a huge part in the history of rock and blues
thanks to Tom Wittrock

1956 1964 1956 from Vic DaPra. The Gibson answer to the popularity of the Fender solid bodied guitars. First came the Goldtops up to 1958 and then the Sunbursts from 1958 to 1960

1966 SG Standards with the elusive Custom finishes
Not all Gibson guitars were Sunburst and Goldtop
Well Strung Guitars

1969 Gibson Byrdland and 1964 ES330-TDC-B RaulBarrios

By the late fifties, Gibson had come to terms with the fact that the solid body guitar sector of their business was losing ground, particularly to Leo Fender's modernistic, even futuristic, Stratocaster model, which was undeniably selling well. The only solid guitar that Gibson could put up against it was the range of Les Paul's, albeit now available by this time in four versions: the Standard, the Custom, the Special, and the Junior. Having been around since 1952 the model was starting to look a bit staid and dated, which was reflected in sales that were steadily declining. The then president of Gibson, a true giant of the industry named Ted McCarty, decided to take a totally new look at the solid body, and he came up with four designs that were anything, but guitar shaped. They were named the Explorer, the Moderne, the Flying V, and the Futura. Different they were, a major departure in guitar design, and most of that concept lives with us to this day. As it was to turn out the Futura never progressed beyond the drawing board (until the example below showed up). The shape was merely like a pinched together version of the Explorer with sharper pointy bits, not unique enough to be a separate model, and was shelved, though in actuality the two shapes were incorporated into the final version of what became the Explorer. Although many sources claim that no Modernes were ever built I have had credible evidence that two examples were in fact produced. A prototype of the Explorer was displayed at the 1957 NAMM show, and officially released in 1958, in which year 19 were made, with a further 3 in 1959. Gibson's own factory production records, which sadly are not always totally reliable, indicate that 98 Flying V's were made in '58 and '59. With the benefit of hindsight, it could be argued that these unconventional body shapes were ahead of their time. They didn't sell initially and stories abound about how Ted McCarty was carrying unwanted Moderne and Explorer bodies out into the Parsons Street factory car park, piling them up and setting fire to them. As the years passed however tastes changed, and guitarists, normally a very conservative bunch, warmed to these new designs. As a result of this growing demand, Gibson went into full production mode on the Flying V, and in due course, it became favoured by many big names, such as Lenny Kravitz, Dave Davies, Lonny Mack, Marc Bolan, Albert King, and scores of others. In 1986 the Gibson Custom Shop made a left handed example for Paul McCartney. So therefore, to coin a phrase, it had truly taken off, though it had taken a while. Reissues, limited editions, and so on have appeared many times since the guitar's introduction, and it has become an established member of the Gibson range. One variation I can't resist recalling was the Flying V-2, which featured those weird boomerang pickups and was produced from 1979 until 1982 during the Norlin era. I think of that guitar as being like a pet tortoise. It wasn't very attractive to look at, and it didn't do much, so why bother? Probably the first time that the Explorer became widely known was when Eric Clapton appeared with one in the Musicman amplifier catalogs, of which he was an endorsee in the early '70s. They became more popular following that exposure, and yet more reissues and limited runs occurred as a result. The guitarist of U2, The Edge, has become closely identified with the model. Gibson's budget range, Epiphone, also features Flying V's and Explorers. The rather extreme shapes have become embraced by the heavy metal crowd, though Ted McCarty had no concept of heavy metal and is probably spinning in his grave.

This is the original owner of the Futrura prototype Ponty "Guitar" Gonzales Jr. with the guitar as it was discovered. Ponty bought the guitar around 1958 from the Gibson salesman who was travelling across the country by train with a selection of samples to sell and take orders. He recalls that he was also offered what may have been the Moderne prototype when he purchased this from the Gibson rep. The guitar eventually ended up in the back window of his Cadillac for 2 decades, the finish being burned by the sun. Kurt Linhof bought the guitar from Ponty in the late '70s by which time it was being stored in a trash bag on his porch. It's identifiable as being the same guitar shown in 1957 NAMM photos by the shadow of the (now missing) logo plate on the headstock and the fact the pickguard was glued on rather than screwed

thanks to Kurt Linhof and Willie Smith

1965 Reverse Firebird III
Otherwise all 1964 appointments' NON-reverse headstock 1 11/16" nut, nickel hardware, neck-through-body construction and 17 degree headstock angle. All original and very rare. This variant was never offered in any Gibson catalogs.
thanks to Mogens Pederson

Gibson made a variety of neck configurations, including their most popular model the 6/12. There were also six string and four string bass versions, six string and six string bass versions, and six string plus mandolin versions. Gibson's double neck guitars were first seen back in the '50s, the body style at that time featured a much deeper body with flat sides, in the manner of a Les Paul body. The one pictured here is the later, and still current, post 1961 expanded SG body style. Despite their considerable mass and weight, these have been popular for over 70 years.

thanks to Viktor Nemeth

1961 Gibson Les Paul SG Custom
in factory Black
Well Strung Guitars

1959 Les Paul Standard
The Paul Kossof Burst
ex Arthur Ramm
and now with Kris Blakely

1964 ES335 Eric Clapton's shipped 20th May '64, this one 3rd June '64. David Keeling

1960 ES-330 TDN
Dot neck

Bob Wootton

1955 ES-5N
Switchmaster
ex Chet Atkins

Simon White

1959 ES-335

thanks to Guitar Point

This 335 sports a retro fitted Bigsby vibrato. The holes are visible where the original tailpiece has been removed. When a Bigsby was factory fitted those holes would always be covered by a black and white plaque with the words Custom Made engraved on it"

1957 ES 225 TD
Ordered from Gibson in1957 and came out with factory PAFs (instead of the standard P90s for the model), parallelogram fretboard inlays and Keystone tulip tuners. Standard inlays for the ES 225 were always dot inlays and standard tuners had oval shaped keys.
Owner- Carlos Pellot
Factory Order Number- U 3213 32
Photo Credit - Raul J. Barrios

1964
Gibson Thunderbird II
Polaris White # 217684

1966
Gibson Thunderbird IV
Pelham Blue

thanks to Craig Brody

1965 Gibson EB-2
Argentine Gray
1 of only 2 known to exist in this color.

1960/1 EB6 #3555
67 shipped before they changed from ES to SG style body PAF guitar pickup. The EB6 completed the semi-hollow line-up for the 1960 Gibson catalogue.

thanks to Craig Brody

thanks to Dave Keeling

1968 EBS-1250 original Black finish thanks to Well Strung Guitars

1958 Gibson Flying V

An original first batch example. The myth-The Legend-The Holy Grail. This guitar has quite an interesting history. It was featured in the 1994 edition of the famous book "Gibson Electrics" by the late Andre Duchossoir. It was believed for many decades that it was one of the V's that was shipped in early 1960 but that is not the case. It's a first batch '58 which possesses all of the features that are common to the first production run. It is logged in the 1958 Gibson factory ledgers and has been confirmed by them as having been shipped on May 26th, 1958, the customer being recorded as the Dixie Bargain Center in Maryland. Just as in Duchossoir's book it now has an early 60's ABR-1 bridge with nylon saddles, and control knobs which were added sometime later. The machine heads were also replaced, but all of those old parts now reside in the original case. "Dixie" has the mix of an early black pickguard and a white jack socket plate.

Courtesy Viktor Nemeth.

CHUCK BERRY

This is Chuck Berry, the undisputed king of rock and roll guitar. His contribution to the music, and the prominence of the electric guitar, is incalculable. Although he owned and used many guitars during his lengthy career, it all began with a Kay Thin Twin K-161, and he soon moved on to the Gretsch 6130 Roundup as seen in the famous 1955 Maybelline video. Soon afterward he purchased the iconic blond Gibson ES350, which he played until 1958 or so when their ES345 and ES355 models were introduced. These remained his mainstay until his death, and his favourite walnut '70s example was buried alongside him.

RIP.

Chuck Berry performing "Roll Over Beethoven," with a display of powerful riffs and charismatic showmanship The audience were typical of that era and just looked on in astonishment. The song stands as a defiant anthem of the rock 'n' roll revolution which was challenging the musical establishment
Johnnie Johnson on piano, Willie Dixon on bass, and Fred Belew on drums

THE SCHNEIDER- RIO

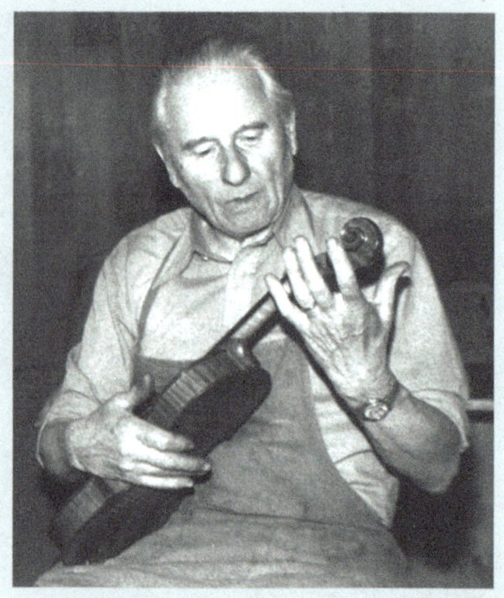

I'm sure many readers will be curious to discover what was happening apropos electric guitars on the other side of the pond while all that exciting stuff was going on in America. The music scene in Europe between the wars was a vibrant one, but different. Traditional music genres held sway, polka bands in Germany and Austria, Gypsy jazz in France, English and Irish folk music, and so on. On the upside, however, bebop jazz was starting to catch on, traveling minstrel shows were increasingly popular, and even more exotic things like Hawaiian music were gaining ground. So who started off the electric guitar explosion? Here's the answer. In a town named Basel in Switzerland there lived a man named Karl Schneider. He was born in 1905 and was apprenticed at a young age to a violin maker. His apprenticeship was completed when he was 23 and he went to work at an instrument maker in Basel called Musikhaus Meinel. As interest in classical violins gradually declined he decided to make guitars, as such instruments were becoming more popular. In 1930 he was selling his first acoustic guitars which bore the Grando label. In 1938 or thereabouts, sources vary, an imported American made arch top jazz guitar was brought to him for repair. Always having had a great interest in engineering and electronics he repaired the guitar, but not before taking note of how it worked and how it was built. He made his own as a result of what he'd learned, and that was Europe's first electric guitar. Sadly they never went into full production, and, Schneider's prototype remains a one-off, for a little while longer anyway. There was then a break in the story due to the war. Despite the fact that Switzerland was neutral, war related work still had to be done. We pick up the story in 1945, by which time Schneider has parted ways with Meinel and was making both acoustic and electric archtop guitars under the Rio brand. Rio did well in what was a relatively sparsely populated market, and by the 1960s he was producing about 1000 guitars per year. Then the same thing happened to Rio that happened to everyone else in the '70s, the tsunami of cheap Japanese guitars. Rio struggled on until 1982 when the factory closed for good. Schneider himself returned to violin making which continued until he died in 1998 aged 93.

thanks to Andrej Abpanalp for this photo. Historian and communications chief of the Swiss National Museum.

Rio

110
120

Nr. 110
Elektrische Hawaii-Gitarre, braun mit weißem Rand, neuestes verstellbares Magnet-Agregat mit abgestufter Tonabnahme, Lautstärkeregler und Tonblende.

No. 110
Guitare électrique hawaienne, brune avec bord blanc, tout nouvel aimant-agrégat mobile avec diminution graduée du ton, réglage du haut-parleur et sourdine.

Nr. 120
Dito, braun mit breitem Rand, Griffbrett und Agregatschutz aus Plexiglas, Einzel-Mechanik.

No. 120
Dito, brun avec bord large, touche et agrégat-protecteur en verre incassable, chaque mécanique à part.

The Grando electric from the 1930s

THE USA TRADE EMBARGO AND THE FIRST LONDON IMPORTS

The US/UK trade embargo was instigated in late 1945 and was a way of addressing the trade balance issue that resulted from the UK having to repay millions built up during the Lend-Lease arrangements that became essential during WWII. It cost the UK millions, and the country was virtually bankrupt at that time, and years of austerity was one result. No USA made goods were allowed into the UK during the period that this was in force. This included things like meat products, steel, machine tools, cars, phonograph records, and of course guitars. A few did make their way over here, either by British musicians who were working there on exchange contracts, who would buy a guitar and bring it back, or some purchased by sailors, either Royal or Merchant Navy, who would buy a guitar and bring it back to sell in the hope of making a little money. Such instances are fairly rare, but they did happen. It was well known for example that sailors would return to Liverpool bringing with them armfuls of rare rock and roll and blues records giving young musicians in Liverpool, and London, access to music that would otherwise have been unavailable to them. John Lennon, amongst many others, cites this as the way he developed a love of such music, and that was the genesis of his career.

The trade embargo was finally lifted in June of 1959, and American made goods of all kinds flooded into the UK market, such was the significant pent up demand. Cars especially sold well, and during that time, and well into the '60s, Buicks, Cadillacs, Chevrolets and US made Fords were a common sight on British roads. Some years ago I used to deal a lot in used American cars and I always wondered why there were so many '59s around but no '58s. Now I know.

American guitars became available too. As you are aware Selmers were the UK importers and wholesale agents for Gibson,Rosetti had Epiphone, Dallas (later Dallas Arbiter) had Fender, and Rose Morris picked up Rickenbacker in the early '60s. I don't think that Guild or Mosrite even had an importer at this time, and I really can't recall now who imported Gretsch or Harmony, though I know somebody did, I remember seeing them on shop walls. The big retailers around the country, like Barratts Of Manchester, Kitchens of Leeds or J G Windows in Newcastle, immediately began to buy in the odd Gibson or Fender or two, found that they would sell quickly, then bought in a load more. And so the UK guitar business grew and grew quickly. By the early '60s, and especially during the Merseybeat boom, any band worth it's salt had ditched their Watkins Rapiers, Framus's and Hofners (mostly) and were sporting Gibson's, Gretsch's, and Rickenbackers.

Aside from those big Rio jazz guitars the first European electric guitars to appear were made by German maker Framus in 1958, with designs aimed firmly at the growing beat group market. Others quickly followed and it wasn't long before guitars such as Fenton-Weill, designed by Jimmy Burns, appeared, and soon after his own Burns brand guitars, Vox's, and Watkins Rapiers amongst others. Guys like me had to use them as that was all we could get at the time. There was a big influx of German guitars other than Framus, made by firms such as Hofner. Hoyer. Hopf, Hohner, (why do they all start with H?), Futurama guitars from Czechoslovakia, Hagstroms and Levins from Sweden, Rosettis and Egmonds from Holland, and Eko and Welson guitars from Italy. Virtually all of them were total rubbish, near impossible to play, sounding even worse, and were certain to quickly quash any hope of a young guitar player having a career. Despite quality issues, all of those companies were producing electric guitars by the early sixties, mostly designed along tried and tested American patterns, and due to the new American competition once the embargo was lifted quality did improve dramatically, in most cases at least.

America is where the market was, and is, and guitar production in Europe would never achieve globally significant numbers. We did however see the rise of smaller, even previously one off custom builders, expanding their production to gain a foothold in the mass market, particularly since the '70s and up to the present time, and here I'm name-checking makers such as Manson, John Birch. Gordon Smith, Pangbourne, Patrick Eggle, Overwater, Tony Zemaitis, and others, and in Germany more recent brands such as Nick Huber. European makers have come a long way since a wobbly start 60 plus years ago. Regrettably, I can't examine them individually in more detail, but there were simply too many and I'd need another volume to do them justice.

The rest, as they say, is history.

A few of the West End stores - Selmer's and Macari's were on Charing Cross Road. Most were to be found in Denmark St. Not shown were Sound City - Shaftesbury Avenue, Lew Davis, and Scarths, both of whom were on Charing Cross Road. Fender Soundhouse - Soho Square, Ivor Mairants Rathbone Place (just off Oxford St). All within a small radius and a mecca for guitarists. It isn't the same vibe these days but there are still quite a few good stores in Denmark St. for the careful buyer.

The UK in the '50s and early '60s

What musical instrument factories there were certainly built guitars, but in the main they would have been gut strung classical Spanish guitars (nylon strings were not invented until 1948) but my research hasn't revealed any evidence at all of electric guitar production until the late 50's. The Swedish maker Hagstrom is often cited as the first European maker to produce an electric guitar in 1958. These were sold in the US bearing the Goya brand. In addition, most instrument factories concentrated on building violins, mandolins, and other stringed instruments. The guitar was not massively popular in those days, and as far as those factories were concerned, somewhat of an afterthought. The Allied bombing during the war of course destroyed many cities, and towns in Germany, and the factories within. It was many years before all of that destruction could be repaired, and the country's infrastructure, to enable factories to resume production. By the late '50s and early '60s, we began to see new guitar production emerge. There were also major producers in eastern Europe, notably Czechoslovakia, where the Futurama branded guitars were produced. Maccaferri are especially of note as their D sound hole Gypsy jazz guitars were favoured by virtuoso guitarist Django Reinhardt who put solo guitar on the map. He was known to have played electric guitar in the late '40s and before he died in 1953 but will always be remembered for his unique style of gypsy jazz with the Maccaferri guitar.

1960 Resonet Grazioso Futurama III - Before the Stratocaster appeared this was the instrument everyone wanted. It was modern looking with great pickup selectors but boasted a poor trem system and poor neck with a hard action.

Hagstrom Futurama II deluxe
thanks to Phils Vintage Guitars

The real revolution would happen with Hank Marvin and his Fender Stratocaster brought to the UK by Cliff Richard. The impact on the young players was sensational. Cliff was the first UK artist to successfully take on the USA pop stars together with The Shadows as his backing band. They had huge sales of singles and LPs, paving the way for what was to come. The photos below show the transition from the equipment available at the beginning of the '60s and the emerging USA imports.

The Images from Edinburgh UK with typical equipment used by UK bands in the early '60s. Ash Gupta (Watkins Rapier Westminster amp and Binson Echo), Douggie McKenzie (1962 Hofner Verithin Vox AC 30), Alan Bell (Hofner bass/pretend Fender piggyback/Linear 30 and Fane 15" speakers).

1964 The Sundowners from Falkirk, Scotland. (1 to r) John McKinlay (Fender Strat-Vox AC30), Brian Watters (Fender Strat-Vox AC30-Watkins Copycat), Andy Hepburn Vocals, Derek Cowan (Rogers Drums), Derek Watters (Framus Bass, Selmer Goliath Treble and Bass), Ian Thomson (Fender Esquire-Vox AC30).

Hofner Committee 1958
Denmark St Guitars

Hofner President 1956

A gallery of the Hofner range of guitars used by the early pop groups in the UK. The thinline Verithin introduced in 1961/2 would be the UK's answer to the Gibson 335 and was probably the best available option to the long suffering UK's guitarists.

1959 Hofner Club 60
Willie Smith

Germany's answer to the Fender Stratocaster and much loved in the UK
The Hofner Galaxie
ATB Guitars

A typical UK working band in 1964 with a variety of instruments and amplifiers
Burns Splitsonic, Epiphone Rivoli, and Hofner Verithin (David Plues).
Vox AC 30s, Wem Copicats, and Burns Orbit 2.
Adrian Kaye and the Impacts performing at Bridlington Spa, UK

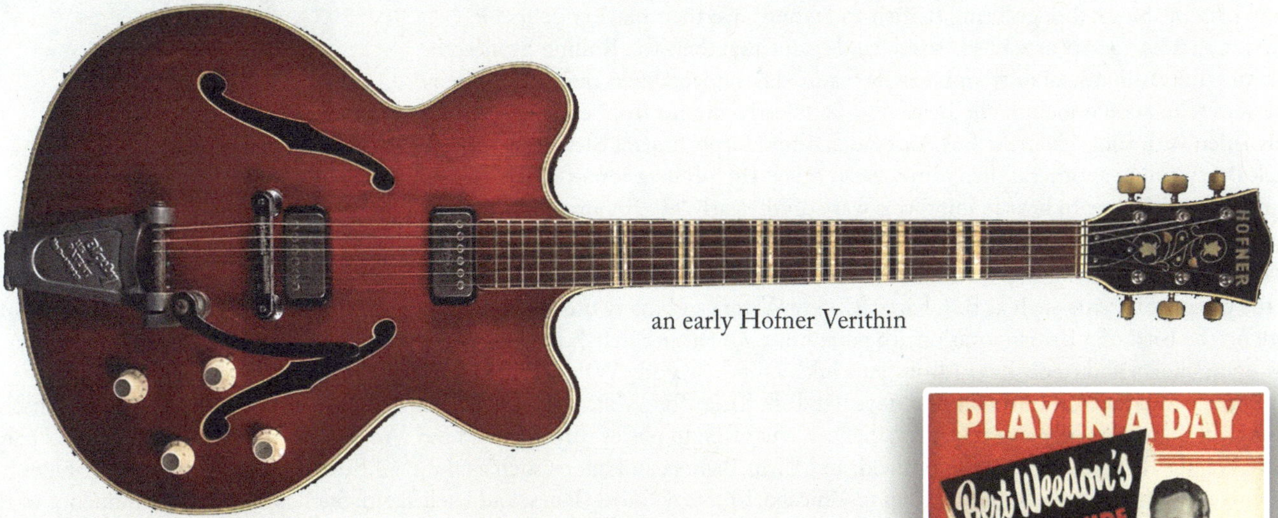

an early Hofner Verithin

Watkins Rapier

The UK in the '50s and early '60s

Something earthshaking happened in the UK during the late 1950s and early 1960s, and it presents us with a question that nobody has ever had an adequate answer for, but it was as if a switch was flipped in the brains of almost every guitarist in the nation. American jazz, blues, and R&B records had been filtering their way into the UK during that period, surreptitiously at first, but after mid '59 by more conventional and legal methods. They found a ready and eager audience, and small specialist record stores started to pop up in places like Liverpool, Newcastle, Manchester, and London which sold such rarities. For us, it was as if a door had been opened into a new world, and British guitar players embraced this imported blues music and took to it as if it were mother's milk. Must be something mysterious in the British psyche. Whatever the reason it kicked off a revolution.

For the sake of younger readers, or our friends over there on the other side of the pond, it would be helpful if I put the '50s British pop scene into context. My memory of the music coming out of the family radio consists of David Whitfield, Alma Cogan, Lita Roza, or Dickie Valentine. It was all vacuous and forgettable. What imported American music there was consisted mainly of Liberace and Rosemary Clooney. All fairly dismal. It got even worse later on when that Godawful skiffle arrived. The dear old BBC was somewhat tardy in giving us teens the new music coming from America, not just rock and roll, but blues, R&B, even doo-wop. It was only a matter of time however before rumours spread, we went to those little shops and started to spend our paper round money on LPs with intriguing and exotic covers. We'd excitedly take these priceless artifacts home, gingerly place them on the turntable, and absorb the sounds of John Lee Hooker, B.B. King, Buddy Guy, and scores of others. It was like music from another world, which in a way it was. To us, Chicago might as well have been on another planet. Being exposed to Muddy Waters and others for the first time was a revelation. Here was music that was raw, real, intense, and exciting, at last something with meat on the bones. Down in leafy Surrey guys like Jeff Beck, Jimmy Page, and Eric Clapton were crouched over their guitars learning all this amazing music, as were others like Keith Richards, Dave Kelly, John Mayall, Alexis Korner, original Stones guitarist Dick Taylor, and yes, even me. It's difficult now to put into words what it was like to hear Howling Wolf's Evil (Chess records 1954) for the first time, or Smokestack Lightning (Chess records 1956). It demonstrated to us a whole new way of using the guitar and then having to learn the techniques necessary to get those authentic sounds. In the fullness of time all of those players did learn to play the blues, though being British and white gave their playing definable nuances. Also, as time passed new blues based bands came together, The Rolling Stones, the Yardbirds, and The Animals, all of whom heavily featured American blues material in their stage repertoires. You could include the Beatles too, and early albums from each of those bands are heavily laden with songs from Arthur Alexander, Slim Harpo, Barret Strong, Bo Diddley, and Chuck Berry amongst others. Then came the so called British invasion of 1964. Things are different now, but you have to bear in mind this was still the early '60s. In any event, long story short. black music performed by white British groups reinvigorated interest in such music. You could even say it was rediscovered by a new more liberal generation. One effect of all of that was that the careers of artists such as B.B. King. Muddy Waters and many others entered a new phase, and they began to sell a lot of records. all on the back of a British invasion. To paraphrase something that B.B. King once said. "If it wasn't for the Rolling Stones, I'd still be doing nickel and dime gigs in Louisiana juke joints". Muddy Waters said something broadly similar. Pretty soon a new American blues boom had got into gear, and guys like B.B. King, The Wolf, Otis Rush, John Lee Hooker, and others found themselves doing European tours to wildly appreciative audiences, and often to places further afield too. We also saw the rise of white blues players like Johnny Winter Ry Cooder, Mike Bloomfield, and Elvin Bishop, and bands such as the Paul Butterfield Blues Band. The blues had come full circle, from the Mississippi Delta, up to Chicago, to sleepy Surrey lanes, and back again. Such is the massive influence of this genre and its infinite variations, that it remains dominant to this day, and players such as Joe Bonamassa, Derek Trucks, Jackie Venson, George Thorogood, and scores of others, keep the flag flying. Buddy Guy seems to be doing pretty well too. The British bands were a little baffled when their American fans began asking them where their music had come from. Had they written it all themselves? When they replied "No, that's a Muddy Waters number", the fan might respond "Who?". The truth was that all of those records were essentially race records, played exclusively on black radio stations, so white people had little or no exposure to the music of black origin prior to the early '60s.

John Mayall

The Rolling Stones playing iconic guitars of that era. Keith Richards with the Gibson Les Paul Standard '59 Burst which would create a huge interest in that model. Andy Summers and Eric Clapton would later use these guitars to great effect. Brian Jones had great taste in guitars and looked the part with the Vox Teardrop. In this photo, Bill Wyman looked slightly incongruent with his choice of Framus bass.

British Rock Group "The Rolling Stones"
LONDON, ENGLAND - CIRCA 1965: British Rock Group "The Rolling Stones" perform on a TV Show
Left to right: Bill Wyman, Brian Jones, Mick Jagger, Charlie Watts, Keith Richards. (Photo by Cyrus Andrews/Michael Ochs Archives/Getty Images)

The continuing story of the electric bass

Leo Fender is generally credited with manufacturing the first bass guitar with his Precision Bass which hit the market in 1951. He'd taken the format of the Esquire and Broadcaster, extended the simple slab body to accommodate the longer scale length, added a low camber fretted maple neck and a single pickup. No pogo stick, however. His claim to being the first is still hotly debated. There was no doubt though that it was a success and through the fifties, all other brands had included at least one bass guitar in their ranges. Gibson stuck to a more conservative approach, and their solid violin shaped EB1 appeared in 1953, with a pogo stick.

Probably the most iconic and recognizable bass guitar ever made was the Hofner Violin Bass, officially designated 500/1, and was the favoured axe of Paul McCartney from his earliest Beatle days to the present. This had virtually the same dimensions as the EB1 but had a hollow body, hence it was much lighter with a softer tone range. This guitar also stuck to a safe traditional style and was first introduced in 1955, though it took a Beatle to really popularize it. The so called Beatle Bass continues in production to this day.

The Kay K162 turned up in 1952, without pogo stick, then the Rickenbacker 4000, a couple of Danelectros including the famous 1958 Longhorn, and the narrow neck Fender Jazz Bass in 1960. Gibson's first semi-hollow bass, the EB2, together with its Epiphone twin, the Rivoli bass, were made available in 1958, and the solid EB0, in its first version, in 1959. Incidentally, all of Gibson's basses were short scale until the Thunderbird was made in 1963, and all Fender basses were long scale until their Mustang of 1966. The Ampeg AUB-1 was mentioned earlier, with pogo stick. The first Gretsch, the shorter scale Bikini bass came out in 1961, and the hollow bodied 6070 in 1962. This was a seriously big instrument for a bass guitar, extra-long scale, a headstock like a shovel, and altogether somewhat of a monster. For those players still reluctant to desert their old habits completely it too came with a pogo stick, but it was the last of the breed. Bassists today can choose from instruments with four strings, five strings, six, eight and even twelve strings. Also, there are fretted and fretless instruments, plus long scale or short scale. Advances in amplification mean that they can at last be heard.

Hofner '56 Violin Bass
Denmark St Guitar

Hofner '59 Violin Bass

Paul McCartney SAP Center in San Jose California during his Freshen Up Tour, with his trusty 1963 Hofner Bass (July 10, 2019)

Performing "Helter Skelter"

Brian Ray is pictured behind him using his custom '62 SG Junior

The Hofner Violin bass would become one of the world's most famous bass guitars and used extensively by Paul McCartney throughout his spectacular career.
photo credit: www.jamesliverani.com

EPIPHONE - THE KALAMAZOO YEARS

By the mid 1950s, Epiphone found themselves mired into an uphill struggle. In the prewar years, they had been the market leaders, on top of their game, producing fine quality arch top jazz guitars and other instruments easily the equal of any of the competition around at that time. Twenty years is a long time in the guitar world however, and what with slowly losing sales volume to their arch rivals Gibson, having had many of their top craftsmen poached by the new Guild company, and having a catalog full of dated guitar designs that were looking a bit long in the tooth, sales had slumped. They were also tardy in introducing instruments to rival those new flashy solid body Fender Stratocasters and Telecasters, not to mention Gibson's best selling Les Paul Gold Tops. Customer demand in those formative rock and roll years was prompting fundamental changes in the industry. In short, Epiphone was out of touch, their race was run, and in 1957 the company was purchased by CMI, Chicago Musical Instruments, who had already been Gibson's parent company since 1944. Interestingly, instead of stubbing out the rival brand forever, which they could so easily have done, Gibson decided to begin manufacturing Epiphone brand guitars in the Kalamazoo factory, and, with some minor tweaks and cosmetic variations, offered Epiphone as an additional line, which would it was hoped expand their customer base. Epiphone after all was a long established and well respected name on guitar headstocks all across America. That's exactly what they did.

As you are all no doubt aware all Epiphone guitars produced during this period with certain exceptions such as the Professional, the Howard Roberts, and the Al Caiola, had a direct equivalent, or twin brother, in the Gibson range. Here are examples of each Epiphone followed by its closest Gibson equivalent - Crestwood/SG Standard, (there was also a Crestwood 12 string which had no Gibson twin until the limited run of SG Standard 12's made around 15 years ago), Crestwood Deluxe/SG Custom, Wilshire/SG Special (though Wilshires were made either with P90's or mini humbuckers), Coronet/SG Junior, Olympic/ Melody Maker, Riviera/ES335 (both were also made in 12 string versions), Casino/ES330 (the Casino had chrome pickup covers and the 330 black plastic. Single pickup versions also made), Sheraton/ES355 Mono, Newport Bass/EB0, Embassy Bass/EB3, Rivoli Bass/EB2, maybe a bit of a stretch but the Windsor and Sorrento models had echoes in Gibson's ES125 and ES225 models though there were several variations over time, Zephyr /ES350, Granada/ES120. A wider range of custom colors were available on Epiphone's solids, and colors such as California Coral or Sunset Yellow were unique to that series though white, Cardinal Red and Pelham Blue were not.

There were full bodied jazz guitars made during these years too, such things had been Epiphone's stock-in-trade after all, which relied largely on the original patterns and molds bought with them from the old plant, but Gibson's own guitars were not so closely comparable with these, thus direct twins are not as obvious. The Emperor was certainly similar to Gibson's ES5 Switchmaster, and the Broadway quite akin to the ES175, but there were significant differences in body outline thus it would be inaccurate to describe them as twins, distant cousins more like.

1961 Epiphone Sheraton
ex G.E. Smith

thanks to Well Strung Guitars

EPIPHONE - THE KALAMAZOO YEARS

Gibson and CMI were taken over by the Norlin Group in 1969 and in 1970 the decision was made to cease all Epiphone production at Kalamazoo, though it should be pointed out that production numbers had already been gradually cut back for a few years previously. All future production was to be in Japan, and the sojourn of the Epiphone brand in Kalamazoo was ended. Nothing more than a blink of an eye in the more than a century long history of the marque, but during that short time some of their most iconic instruments were produced which have subsequently become sought after collectors' items. The next chapter in the brand's history is a different story and a bit of a rocky one at that. It takes us from Japan, via South Korea, and finally to China, where today most Epiphone guitars are made at their own dedicated factory, aside from a limited USA series which are made at Gibson's factory, now relocated to Nashville. The current Chinese made range is extensive, including not only certain original Epiphone models but reproductions of Gibson classics too, which are referred to as their "Inspired By Gibson" series. There are Firebirds, whole ranges of ESs, SGs, a plethora of Les Pauls, a 6/12 Twin Neck, plus Flying V's, all available at very agreeable prices.

The facing page shows six photographs, generously submitted by dedicated collectors, displaying the cream of Epiphone's output during the period in which they were made alongside Gibson's own branded instruments at the Parsons Street plant. Starting from top left to right we have an Al Caiola, a '65 Riviera, '66 Pelham Blue Casino. Below, left to right, a Cherry Red Rivoli, Tan Casino and finally the 1961 ES-230T The USA Epiphones remain a great entry point to the vintage market but price are rising rapidly.

thanks to Gary Dick for this sunburst Casino

Al Caiola

1964/5 Riviera
author

1966 Pelham
Blue Casino
anaon.

1967 Rivoli
thanks to Cosmo

1964 - Tan Casino
thanks toMark Chatfieled

61 ES230T
photo credit Cal Wootton

There were noticeable differences in the basic design between the two lines of solid bodies, and, to be fair, the use of the word "twin" could be misleading, and "comparable" is more accurate. Gibson SGs had the two sharp horns and the chamfered or beveled body while the early versions of Epiphone's solids had a rounder symmetrical body, a bit like a 1960 double cutaway Les Paul Junior that had melted in the heat, and all of these had a three-a-side headstock. In 1963 it was decided to give the range a facelift, and the 1964 catalogue pictures guitars and basses with a new asymmetrical body style and single side "Batwing" headstocks, a format that has persisted to this day. Also notable is the use of the small coil, or mini, humbuckers on many models. Pre merger Epiphones were equipped with a single coil pickup with a metal cover. These are generally referred to as New York pickups. As all of the pole screws were mounted on one side they had the appearance of a mini humbucker, although they were not. Post merger it was thought to be a good idea if as much of the original distinctive look of the guitar was maintained. Allegedly it was Seth Lover who came up with a mini version of his own humbucker specifically for Epiphone which would fit into their models without altering their appearance to any great extent or having to change the tooling on the jigs and pattern makers. They worked very well, though having a smaller coil which required less windings and smaller magnets resulted in a sharper more trebly tone. The mini humbucker was standard equipment on all relevant models from 1961 onwards. Once Epiphone production ended in the '69-'70 model year Gibson found that they had boxes full of these mini units left over, thus it was the Gibson Les Paul Deluxe was introduced as a way to use them all up. There was also a plan to make an Epiphone Les Paul Standard. This would have been identical to the '58 to '60 run of what are now known colloquially as Bursts but would have had a double cutaway body outline. I once had a photo of noted guitar collector Robert Johnson holding one, but it has now unfortunately been misplaced. In any event, the guitar never went into production, and I am reliably informed that only two examples were ever made.

photo credit: Derek Bruneau

photo credit: Edward Lott

1964 Epiphone Coronet: Serial Number 65361
John Shannon

photo credit: Edward Lott

1967 Rickenbacker 325
1990 Rickenbacker 325
John Lennon LTD edition.

Jacques Menache

1975 Rickenbacker 620.
with a 'one off' Matchless DC 30
from Phil Jamison

1959 Rickenbacker 4000 Bass
Mapleglo # B9140
1 of 50 ever produced over 5 years.

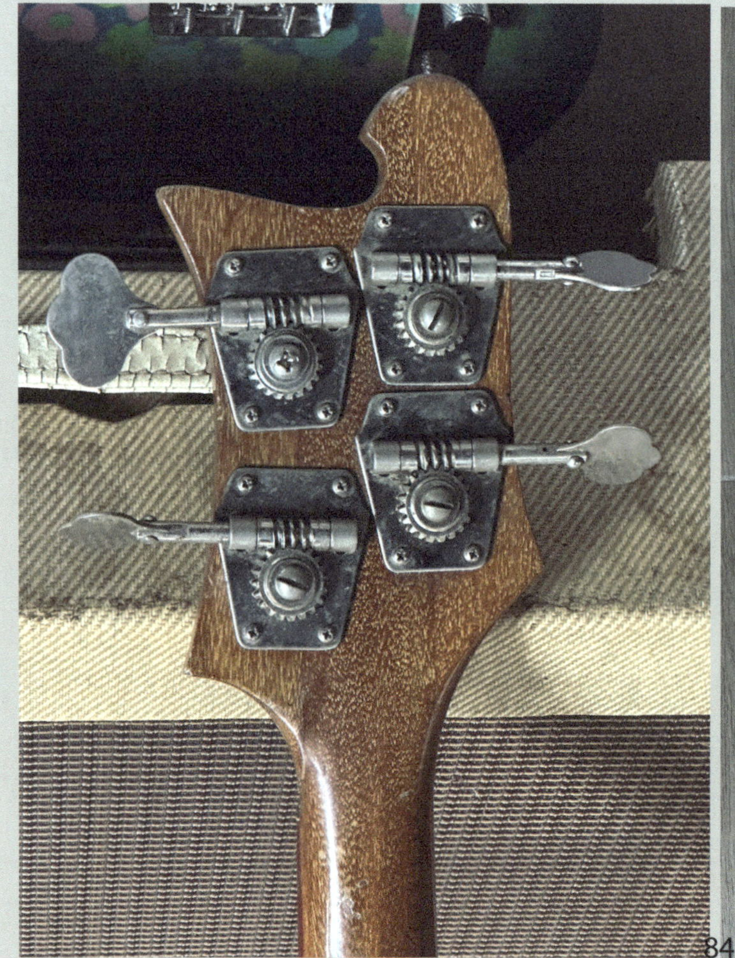

GRETSCH

The Gretsch company has been mentioned several times elsewhere in this volume, but nowhere near often enough as Gretsch was a major player and one of the Big Six so therefore deserves far more column inches. Over the years much has been committed to print describing Gretsch guitars, indeed a handful of books have been written dedicated to this brand specifically. As my space here is limited I cannot hope to compete with those fine and authoritative works, nor would I wish to, so what I intend to achieve here is to offer a general overview, illustrated with a few photographs of especially worthy examples of Gretsch craftsmanship.

The history of the company is a long one, extending far beyond the one hundred year remit of this book, so as far as those beginnings are concerned here are the bare bones. Friedrich Gretsch came to America from Germany in 1883, settled in Brooklyn, and began to manufacture banjos, drums, and tambourines. Friedrich died suddenly in 1895 aged a mere 39 and the firm passed down to the next generation, which happened to be his then teenage son Fred. In 1916 Fred Gretsch moved to a larger factory, a ten story building again located in Brooklyn. At one point they had expanded into four factories scattered across the borough. In 1942 Fred (by now called Fred Sr.) retired and passed the firm along to Fred Jr., who was to navigate the company into the modern era. The family was apparently not imaginative when it came to naming their children. During the war years, Fred Jr. was serving in the navy and his brother William continued to operate the Brooklyn factory. William died in 1948 and Fred Jr. resumed full control.

Fast forward to 1967, and a by now struggling Gretsch company was purchased by Baldwin, at that time the largest musical instrument manufacturing company in the world. In 1969 Baldwin relocated the Gretsch factory, the existing Brooklyn operations having become inconvenient and costly. The chosen new location was in rural Arkansas, and to the town of Booneville. A good home for a guitar company as Booneville was timber country, and the principal industry in the town was timber and sawmills. Their drum factory settled in the small town of DeQueen, about a 100 mile drive south from Booneville. In 1973 the factory was gutted by a major fire and guitar production was disrupted for months afterwards. They had barely got back on their feet when a second fire occurred in 1974. As a result, very few guitars were produced during those two years. In 1983 the giant that had been Baldwin went spectacularly bankrupt. In 1984 Fred W Gretsch, and nephew of Fred Sr., managed to regain control of the company and ownership returned to the family.

In 1989, and in response to the influx of cheaper guitars flooding in from Asia, Fred W did what most other American guitar makers did, and began producing ranges of instruments made in Japan, though US production still continued. In 2002 Fender purchased Gretsch. In a unique arrangement, although Fender was responsible for all of the manufacturing, marketing, and distribution of Gretsch products, Fred W remained the owner of the company ensuring that the 120 year bloodline remained unbroken. Today significant numbers of Gretsch guitars are made in China, a range which includes many of the old favourites or updated versions thereof. Gretsch also have a Custom Shop facility, building top end all American Gretsch guitars, and this facility is shared with Fender's own Custom Shop in Scottsdale Arizona.

During the late 1920s and into the 1930s Fred Sr. was smart enough to observe how guitars were increasing in popularity and the banjo elbowed out into second place. His answer to that was to make less banjos and more guitars. These would have been both flat top round hole acoustics and cello style archtops. As electric guitars gained ground during the '30s Gretsch couldn't avoid the electric bug either, and, as written earlier, the first Gretsch electric was made in 1939. Following the war production of all Gretsch guitars, especially electrics, boomed. It was the golden age. In 1954 famous country guitarist Chet Atkins was brought on board with a view to marketing a range of guitars bearing his name. Chet Atkins was to Gretsch what Les Paul was to Gibson. Big names sell guitars. This transpired however to be a double edged sword, as, due to the Atkins connection, a lot of players perceived Gretsch guitars to be most suitable for country pickers, and rock n rollers didn't buy them, preferring instead to buy Gibsons or Fenders, although there were notable exceptions.

All early Gretschs were fitted with single coil pickups made by DeArmond. There was a lot of gossip going around in the trade about the theory surrounding a new more efficient humbucker pickup, and then employee Ray Butts decided to make one. In 1957 his new humbucker pickup, which Gretsch called the Filtertron, was ready to market. The patent application on his pickup was just beaten to the punch by Seth Lover's unit. Just a couple of months earlier and Ray Butts would have gone down in history instead of Lover. Shown on the next page is not a comprehensive list of every guitar that Gretsch has ever made, but merely a list of the most often seen and popular models made during the company's most prolific years, thus the ones you are most likely to encounter, and their model numbers.

1965 Country Gentleman in Burgundy
Well Strung Guitars

GRETSCH GUITARS

Semi acoustic guitars...
Single Anniversary......6124,
Double Anniversary....6118,
Tennessean.......6119,
Country Club......6193,
Nashville.....6120,
Viking....6187,
Country Gentleman....6122,
Rally........6105,
White Falcon...6136,
Synchromatic.....1627

Solid body guitars..
Corvette 6132

Solid guitars with weight relief chambered bodies....
Duo Jet.... 6128,
Jet Firebird...6131,
Sparkle Jet.....6129,
Roc Jet...7610,
Roundup.... 6130,
Penguin.... 6134

Gretsch guitars were a common sight in the hands of guitarists from '60s British pop and beat groups, such as the Animals, Freddie And The Dreamers, and scores of others. George Harrison was a famous Gretsch user, and his Tennessean has become almost as famous as he was. The then Prince Charles, now King Charles III, got the guitar playing bug too and bought himself a Tennessean. He might possibly still have it tucked away in a palace cupboard somewhere.

One of the most iconic and most famous Gretsch guitars was the so called cigar box guitar played by Bo Diddley. This had an interesting, though painful, birth. Bo was performing one evening with his Gibson L5 when he tripped and fell, trapping the guitar beneath him. He received serious bruising to his "groin area". As a result, he determined to play a guitar with a much smaller body and one that didn't have big curves and bulges that could be potentially harmful. His idea was stunning in its simplicity, just a square box. He took the idea to Gretsch who built one for him. He loved it and was rarely seen without it, or something very similar, in the decades that followed. He was also responsible for designing the Jupiter Thunderbird (6199), based on an idea inspired by a tailfin on a late 50's American car. This model launched in 1959, and one was used by each member of his band, including the 6199B bass version. Billy Gibbons was very enamoured with the whimsical design, and he was seen playing one so often that it eventually became known as the Billy-Bo. Other notable Gretsch players include Stephen Stills who was very attached to his White Falcon, as was phenomenal '50s jazz guitarist Mary Osbourne. Brian Setzer and Eddie Cochran both favoured the 6120 Nashville, and AC/DC's Malcolm Young used a modified 6131 Jet Firebird. Regretfully I'm going to conclude this section of text now as this has the potential to be a very long list. Suffice it to say that a lot of famed players have owned a Gretsch at some point in their careers, understandably so.

thanks to Frank Manno

GRETSCH WHITE FALCON
#13450

This was the first White Falcon built in 1954 designed by Jimmie Webster and displayed at the 1954 NAMM show

In 1955 he gifted it to Mary Osborne. She was at that time (and still is) a renowned jazz guitarist. He signed her to an endorsement contract with Gretsch for photos only. She is seen with this guitar for several print ads for Gretsch over the years. She is also featured with it on the cover of her only LP "A Girl and Her Guitar". This LP was from 1959. There are two covers for this LP. Both featured the Falcon. One was while she was pregnant and the second version after birth and she was slimmed down.

She sold this guitar to a collector Bill Ryan. He purchased the guitar from her in about 1991. She passed in 1992.

1962 Gretsch "Princess" in super rare original Pink with gold hardware. Original white gig bag with gold trim Most of these are white, with very few in Pink and Blue. Based on a single pickup Corvette and finished in pink in an effort to get more girls playing and of course buying guitars. It had very limited success.
Gary Dick

Rob Lurvey

1976 Gretsch (Baldwin) Corvette Deluxe - Model 7632
Cumberland Guitars

Jacques Menache

1955 Roundup #13987, an early example with the steer head inlay on the headstock also cow and cactus inlays plus engravings on the fingerboard, plus the G brand. 1956 6120 #18991 Transitional model with G brand, block inlays - the vibrato unit, it's called the Breakaway Bigsby, It came right after the first units that were made with a fixed arm but before the normal Bigsby units from late 1956, only 19 guitars were made with these vibrato units. The amp is from 1955, # 81419, a 6169 Roundup

Morgens Pederson

SUPRO VALCO & AIRLINE GUITARS

Supro, Valco and Airline are not brands that might instantly leap out at you when you are considering buying a guitar, especially outside of the USA, but however, I suspect that many of you more senior American players might well have begun your musical journeys with a guitar from one of these three budget brands. I have lumped all three together as they ultimately all became part of the same company. The precise beginnings of Supro and Valco seem to be a little misty, however, what we do know is that Valco emerged as a separate entity from its origins concerning the Dobro and National Steel guitar companies which were involved in the manufacture of resonator guitars. Now I haven't previously mentioned resonators as they are not electric, but I have mentioned that dance band guitarists needed more volume. In the early days, prior to the invention of electromagnetic guitar pickups, several guitar makers, such as Ed Dopyera, were experimenting with a metal membrane contained within the guitar body which would vibrate when a string was sounded and was a bit like a reversed speaker cone to look at. The theory was that the cone, or resonator, would produce more volume than a conventional guitar, as indeed it did. Not long after these appeared the electric guitar came along which rendered resonators largely redundant. They did, however, produce a very specific, and unique tone which became very popular, especially with Delta blues guitarists, a good example would be Son House. Thus, they survive to this day. But I digress, and I haven't mentioned the Selmer Maccaferri guitar either, with the phonograph style horn mounted inside it, for the same reason, it wasn't electric. So back to Valco. The company was founded in 1940, and in reality, were intended to be a cheaper offering than the Dobro and National lines. and started guitar production right away, though their first electric-acoustics don't appear until 1944 (allegedly), their initial forays into electric guitar production being amplified versions of existing resonator guitars. Designed from the ground up solid body electrics were still years away. Throughout their history Supro/Valco concentrated on the budget market, a bit more expensive than Silvertone. but way cheaper than Gibson or Epiphone. Supro were already established as an amplifier manufacturer, who incidentally were responsible for making the first ever amplifier with a built in reverb. At some point, though the exact date remains unclear, Valco and Supro merged as a result of National taking over Supro. Fast forward to the '60s, by which time Supro were making guitar bodies from fibreglass, the first to do so, and, as far as I am aware, the last. They were advertised as guitars made from Res-O-Glas, so a gold star for them when it came to the alternative materials experiments. The Supro/Valco company launched their Airline brand in 1958 which was intended to expand their market, lots of bright colours, even stripes, were prominently featured. The Airline catalogue featured the now iconic 'map' guitar. Valco merged with Kay in 1967 but ceased operations the following year. Many of those guitars, still retaining the same designs and features, are currently being produced by the Canadian based Eastwood company, so you can still buy them, if you want something that looks vintage, or simply out of nostalgia. Supro brand amps are also still being made to very high standards.

Formed in 1942, Valco were the cornerstone of affordable guitar building in the post war era. Responsible for building solid body guitars for both National and Supro (both companies having close ties to Valco), the Belmont was introduced alongside the more popular Dual Tone. It came with either a neck or bridge pickup and Valco's Kord King neck which featured a large metal section along its full length instead of the truss rod.

1955 El Capitan Electric Archtop

thanks to Imperial Vintage Guitars

WASHBURN & MOSRITE GUITARS

The Washburn brand was the trademark and marketing name of guitars made by Lyon and Healey, who had been making guitars and other instruments since 1864, though the Washburn brand name only began to be used in 1888. They produced a large range of fine quality guitars and other fretted instruments and established themselves as a major name in the industry over the following decades, and well into the 20th century. I find it surprising therefore that they didn't produce any electric guitars at all until 1978, way behind almost everyone else, and even then they were made in Japan. I was working in a guitar store at that time, and I can well recall unpacking the first shipment and trying them out. Although unremarkable in general appearance they did have one notable feature. They featured a neck through body design, somewhat akin in principle to the '63 to '65 series of Gibson's Firebird guitars. It was easy to grasp the theory, that being that if you had one continuous length of wood, to which were fitted the machine heads, fretboard, pickups, bridge and tailpiece, you would, in theory at least, then have the maximum amount of sustain and tuning stability, as the sounding length of the string was not interrupted by a change in the wood or it's grain, as a bolted on Fender neck would be, or even a set glued in neck, like Gibson, Gretsch and almost everybody else.

There were, and are, many innovators and geniuses associated with the guitar industry, and Semie Moseley is right up there with the best of them. An ex Rickenbacker employee he started building his own guitars as early as 1952, then honing his skills on his iconic twin neck models beginning around 1954. By 1956 he was financially in a position to start his own company proper, and that became the Mosrite company. Famously some of his earliest twin necks were made for the late Larry Collins, a child guitar prodigy, massively popular in the 50's, and beyond. Those guitars generally had one standard six string neck, and one six string octave guitar neck. At least one featured single side headstocks, and other examples feature three a side headstocks which would become the standard on his later models. Mosrite also built twin necks for country guitar virtuoso Joe Maphis, and his popularity immensely helped launch the Mosrite guitar brand name into the mainstream. A range of artist endorsed Joe Maphis models were eventually produced. I was fortunate enough to own a Mosrite twin neck for a while back in the 70's, and it was a great guitar, metallic blue being an added bonus, and I wish I had it now. All Mosrite guitars were notable for two major design features. The first was the body styling. Not only was it unusual, almost looking as if had been made back to front, the right hand bout longer than the left hand, additionally the body had a feature referred to as the German Carve, an idea Moseley had gained (stolen?) from Roger Rossmeisl, who was employed at Rickenbacker during the same period as Moseley. The final body shape, which would persist throughout the guitars history, was quirky though viewed by some as bit of an improvement on Leo Fender's planks of wood. The second was a very low fret profile which, for some players at least, resulted in a very fast action. much loved in later years by Johnny Ramone. It so happened, by sheer chance, that the rise of Mosrites visibility in the guitar landscape of the time coincided with the craze for guitar-led instrumental groups, which itself was to merge withanother craze, surfing music. Instrumental groups abounded, like the Ventures, the Piltdown Men, the Surfaris and the Chantays in the US, various British groups such as the Shadows, the Dakotas, and from Sweden the Spotnicks. Mosrite were ideally placed to capitalize on all of that, and their subsequent association with the Ventures is well known, eventually resulting in an entire line of Ventures model guitars and basses. That association with the whole California twangy guitar era had its short term benefits but ultimately transpired to be somewhat of a poisoned chalice. When that scene had run its course, Mosrites sales slumped. In 1963 the Ventures discontinued their use of Fender guitars and went exclusively to Mosrite until their endorsement contract ended in 1968. As is the way of things the craze for surf music and instrumental groups diminished in the early sixties, and was virtually dead in the water, no pun intended, by the time of the British invasion of 1964. Mosrite struggled on, even introducing new models such as the semi acoustic Celebrity model, based on the format of Gibson's ES335, in the mid '60s, but the salad days were over. Semie Mosely died in 1993, but his particular brick in the guitar Wall of Fame is richly deserved. His unique approach to guitar design and its development should not be understated. The surviving Moseley family, and his descendants, are still building guitars on a one-off custom order basis to this day. Long may they continue.

thanks to Carter Vintage Guitars

1966 "Baritone" Bass. Described as a prototype, this Blue Sparkle could very well be the only six-string Mosrite bass in existence. Six-string basses were never advertised in the Mosrite catalog.

Well Strung Guitars

COLLINGS GUITARS

Bill Collings, a luthier from Ohio with an engineering background, and a part time journalist, was invited by a friend to settle in Houston, which he did, and in 1973 he began to build guitars there, essentially operating as a one-off custom builder. His watchwords were craftsmanship and quality. The guitars he made were complimented highly by several local musicians, and, as so often happens in this industry, his reputation spread, the result being that his production quantities steadily increased. Limited facilities severely restricted his output, however, and Collings, despite making the best of the small number of skilled staff he had, found that the visibility of his brand stubbornly remained very low key. All of this reached the ears of famed guitar dealer and collector George Gruhn, who, in 1987, ordered 25 Collings guitars to retail in his Nashville store. This turned out to be a Big Leap Forward in the presence of the marque on the wider market. Collings simply had to move to a larger premises in order to keep up with the now burgeoning demand, thus it was in 1989 that he moved to bigger premises in Austin TX. Even that plant was eventually outgrown, and a larger factory was found in 1992. This was also in Austin and is where they remain to this day.

As of 2012 the company had 85 employees and completed around 14 instruments a day of varying types. That's around 4000 a year if they don't work weekends. The Colling's current range includes flat top acoustics, archtops, mandolins, ukuleles, and both solid body and semi acoustic electrics. To keep true to the theme of this book we will peruse only their electric guitar range. There are 6 basic models, and taking into account the variations available one potentially would have 25 distinct instruments to choose from. Models include the single cutaway solid 360, the I-35 , shamelessly based on a Gibson ES335, and the SoCo, a single cutaway semi acoustic. Arch top models include the CL-Jazz, available in 16", 17", or 18" lower bout widths, the AT-16, a non cutaway f-hole acoustic, the AT-16DL with a venetian cutaway, and the AT-17, the electric version of the former. In the event that none of those floats your boat, they do have a custom shop. Bill Collings original ethos of craftsmanship and quality are still very much in evidence, no cutting of corners there, but naturally quality costs money, and these guitars aren't cheap, resting confidently and comfortably at the top end of the market. Like anything else in life, you get what you pay for. Bill Collings passed away in 2017 but his name, and the guitars that bear it, will be around for a very long time.

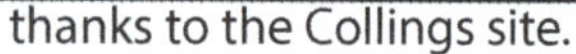

thanks to the Collings site.

While I'm on the subject, and on a personal note, I am very encouraged to observe that the Collings catalogue offers such a large selection of semi acoustic and arch top jazz guitars. They apparently are selling well, and I have a pet theory as to why this would be. All of us baby-boomers, and that includes me, are unavoidably getting older. That youthful rebellion is ebbing away, our testosterone levels are declining, our hair is falling out, and a lifetime of our ear splitting screaming guitar solos are becoming less satisfying, even, dare I say it, mundane. If you are anything like me, you will be discovering that decades of playing in bands performing Blue Cheer covers has mysteriously lost its attraction. In other words, we are slowing down, and a more melodic and ear friendly musical genre begins to appeal. That is quite likely to be jazz. I'm fairly confident therefore that as all of us get into our '60s and even '70s we start listening to Wes Montgomery records and figuring out a new path for the last gasp of our musical careers. That's why I'm so happy to see those jazz guitars, and indeed there does seem to have been a surge in interest in that genre over the past couple of decades which bears out my baby boomer theory. These big old jazz boxes, which occupy a significant market sector, are not just made by Collings of course and there are others on the market, even though, oddly enough, Gibson have discontinued all of theirs, the L5, Byrdland, Super 400, ES175 and others are now history. A couple remain in their little sister Epiphone range, and the current Guild catalogue fortunately features quite a few, and, being now made in China, at a very affordable price. There are a plenty of others dotted around, bearing such brand names as D Angelico, Ibanez, Godin, Eastman, Heritage, The Loar and Peerless,, plus a number of European brands, so there will be something available to suit any of us. Several of those are Chinese made budget priced instruments, though of an extraordinary quality given their low cost, whilst others are the price of a decent secondhand car. If you really want to push the boat out there are many boutique and custom builders around the world who will be glad to make a guitar just for you if price is no object. Lastly, it is striking how similar modern f-hole archtops are to those that were being made a century ago, some of which are pictured in these pages. In fact, they are more or less identical. The guitar has progressed so much over the past 100 years, but the jazz guitar, being such a perfect design, cannot be improved.

City Limits Jazz Sunburst The Fellowship of Acoustics

Ford Thurston with his Collings I-35 LC Vintage.
Photo by Alan Clarke.

GUILD GUITARS

GUILD, A NEW KID ON THE BLOCK GOES GUNNING FOR THE BIG BOYS

The name of Guild has cropped up several times as this book has progressed, but I haven't reviewed the company in any great detail so I will rectify that omission here. Guild became a major player throughout the '50s, '60s, and beyond, and undeniably deserves their seat at the Big Six Annual Christmas party.

The company was founded by Alfred Dronge, a jazz guitarist employed as a session musician in the New York jazz scene of the '30s and '40s. He eventually opened his own music shop in 1945 in partnership with a gentleman named Barney Sagman, the shop trading as Sagman And Dronge, though Dronge bought out Sagman's share in 1947. Alfred carried out regular repair work to instruments brought to him, a major income stream for his fledgling business. He became an expert at examining how the guitars were made and just knew he could do better. In 1952 he joined up with ex Epiphone employee George Mann with the intention of building up his own guitar manufacturing company, still to be in New York which would be named Guild. Dronge just didn't have the same ring about it. One added stroke of good fortune would have been the number of skilled craftsmen that had followed Mann, deserting Epiphone who at the time were involved in a disruptive factory relocation. His first guitars were all archtop jazz guitars, following the tried and trusted Gibson and Epiphone format, and in next to no time had equalled their quality. In 1956 he moved to a bigger factory across the Hudson to Hoboken New Jersey. Also, in 1956 Guild made the first of many artist endorsed models, this one being the Johnny Smith Artist which remained part of the range until 1960. The company made fine quality guitars and output grew rapidly through the remainder of that decade and on into the '60s, arguably Guilds most successful period. Other artist models followed including the Duane Eddy and the George Barnes. Some other notable Guild players have been mentioned elsewhere in these pages.

1958 M75 Aristocrat

The first solid body Guild guitar, the S100 Polara, was introduced in 1963 and was to run, initially, until 1978. Observing it's strong similarity to the Gibson SG Standard was unavoidable. I had an example of the S100 which had acorns and oak leaves carved into the body. I never was quite sure why. A whole slew of thinline semi-acoustic Starfire models were also available on the market st this time. In 1966 Guild was purchased by the Avnet Corporation, an electronics company. Alfred Dronge was kept in place as a company director, thus retaining control over his product. Also in 1966, the factory was relocated once more, this time to a disused furniture factory in Westerly Rhode Island, and it was here. in my view, the company enjoyed its best years. Guild's administrative offices were to remain in Hoboken. Sadly, whilst flying from one location to the other, Alfred Dronge was killed when his plane crashed. He was 60 years old. Control of the company was assumed by Leon Tell. In the UK the importation and distribution of Guild guitars had been patchy, often not existing at all, right through the '50s and '60s, and for that reason, the Guild brand never achieved the market penetration that Gibson or Fender did. In 1973 UK distribution was acquired by Strings And Things, the wholesale arm of Top Gear Music which had a world famous retail shop in London's Denmark Street. For the first time in its history sales of Guild in the UK, and beyond, really took off. Guild's sales manager at that time was the amiable Neil Lillien, and his support was invaluable.

Despite all of that, Guild seemed to struggle and volumes fell far short of making Guild a viable competitor to market leaders Fender or Gibson. The almost inevitable outcome was that Guild was sold to Fender in 1995 and in 2001 production moved to Corona California, marking the end of their Westerly Rhode island period. In 2004 production was moved once again to Tacoma Washington, and in that same year production of all electric guitars ceased. Upheavals continued as in 2014 the Guild brand was sold to the Cordoba company, who up until then had only made high quality classical Spanish guitars. To their credit, Cordoba soon introduced a full line of Guild electrics, the Newark Street series, all of which echoed old favourites, but were now to be made in China. More upset was to come as Cordoba was sold to Yamaha in 2023. Production of Guild electrics guitars continued uninterrupted. The current catalogue features the S100 Polara in eight different finishes, plus a Kim Thayil Artist Edition, plus the relatively recent Surfliner, also in eight finishes, and the old M75 Aristocrat is thankfully also still there. All of the old Starfire models are still being made, including a twelve string, and the Jet 90, a new three pickup variant on the Starfire theme but with a single side headstock. Current jazz models include the Manhattan, Savoy, and the three pickup Switchmaster style Stratford. There is also the T50, an entry level single pickup non cutaway thinline semi, very much like the Epiphone Century. Just a few years ago the catalogue also featured the wonderful and quirky Thunderbird, and the CE100D Capri, one of my most favorite ever guitars, but sadly both of those have now been dropped. So the name of Guild marches on, and the current more affordable range will inject new life into the brand that Alfred Dronge created over 70 years ago. Surely that can only be a good thing.

1961 Guild Starfire III Serial number 17841 1965 Guild Starfire V Serial Number EN-101
1966 Guild Starfire VI Serial Number DB51 thanks to John Shannon

HOWARD ROBERTS

I want to give space, well deserved space at that, to the Epiphone and Gibson Howard Roberts guitars, but first a look at the man himself. Often referred to as the guitarists guitaris't, Howard Roberts (1929-1992) was a prodigy. He started playing guitar at the age of eight, on a cheap Kalamazoo acoustic his parents had given him for Christmas. He displayed a natural aptitude for the instrument, and by the time he was 15 his guitar teacher had to go to Howard's father and tell him, There's nothing more I can teach him, he's better than I am. Playing primarily jazz and blues he gravitated into the LA session musicians scene, most notably with The Wrecking Crew, a club of sorts for LA session players, which also included Tommy Tedesco, and Barney Kessel, with whom he became a great friend and occasional collaborator. The Wrecking Crew will be heard on Phil Spector's records from the early '60s, some of the greatest studio productions ever. Howard's playing will go on to be heard on hundreds of movie and TV themes, far too many to list here, and he can also be heard on recordings by such stars as Peggy Lee, and on to the music from the movie Bullitt. During his career he made 21 solo albums which crossed different genres, from jazz to rock and roll, two of which were released posthumously. An extraordinary CV by any standards.

As many guitarists seem to be he was an obsessive tinkerer, must be something in the DNA, and most of his guitars were modified by him to some degree. Herb Ellis had given Howard an old Gibson ES150, which dated back to the 1930s, and which became his main guitar right through the '50s and '60s. Howard owned several other guitars too, including a Fender Telecaster. He knew, however, that he could come up with something different, better even, and he designed an archtop guitar, but with an oval soundhole in the centre of the table, (that's the technical term for a guitars top) rather than the regular two f-holes. He approached Gibson with the idea and the story goes that Ted McCarty didn't want his production line cluttered up with weird experiments, but there was a small section of the factory currently not in use and contained machinery and tooling which had been used as the production area for the L4. He was welcome to use that, but any guitars made were to carry the Epiphone brand and not Gibson. These stories of course are merely anecdotes but occur in books and on internet sites so regularly that there must be a grain of truth in there. Personally, I wasn't there and everybody who was has long since passed away. After a small number of prototypes had been made production of the guitar that was to become the Howard Roberts model began in the mid '60s. In 1969 the Norlin takeover happened, and the Howard Roberts was rebranded as a Gibson. Very few were made, and some sources claim that 64 of these were shipped. Things start getting a bit murky after that and the truth seems difficult to definitively pin down. I will try to boil down the information that I have into a logical timeline. I have done my absolute utmost to ensure accuracy here, but as so much is contradictory this has presented me with a problem. According to sources Epiphone branded Howard Roberts models were also shipped in '70. They were then discontinued, not reappearing until 1973 as a Gibson. By this time there had been changes. The mini humbucker that was fitted to the original run had been upgraded now to a full humbucker, and, as before, these were suspended as they had been on the Johnny Smith Artist model. The pickups had a bendable metal plate attached to them with four screw holes so it could be attached to the end of the neck. There also was the Howard Roberts Artist model and a Custom model. The Artist was the fancier of the two, having an ebony fretboard and gold plated hardware. All of these featured three controls, one being volume, a second described as a mid-range roll off control, and the third being a treble roll off control. These were made until 1981. It is worth noting that a purely acoustic version of the Howard Roberts was also made. By 1981 extant records indicate that 73 acoustics were shipped and 276 electrics of both types. Then the Howard Roberts Fusion showed up.

The Fusion was a more conventional instrument at first glance. It was not unlike a Gibson ES175 with two normal humbuckers but featured a feedback suppressing centre block which tended to give it a lot more weight than the 175, though the body was slimmer which helped out somewhat. It had a single cutaway which was much deeper and wider than normal, and it had the six prong Goldfinger tailpiece with the small screw adjusters for fine tuning. This guitar appeared in 1979 and initially was offered in ebony or tobacco sunburst. The Fusion was upgraded in 1988 to the Fusion II, which featured pickups designed by Bill Lawrence which had a higher output. A new push-pull volume control gave the player a coil tap option. By '88 the Gibson production had moved to Nashville and the Fusion II was made there. as was the Fusion III, introduced in 1991. There doesn't appear to be any major difference between version II or version III other than the finish options which by now included cherry red. Production of the Fusion III was gradually wound down during the early 2000's and the model had all but vanished by 2005. It was however still in the catalogue as a Custom Shop edition until 2009 when it was finally discontinued. Speaking purely personally I think the Fusion is a fine guitar, extremely versatile, and useful for any genre from jazz to hard rock and I can't understand why they weren't more popular than they turned out to be. All of the Howard Roberts guitars were certainly different, thoughtfully designed, and marked significant advances in guitar design. We can thank the late Howard Roberts for that.

A 1970 Howard Robert's workshop with publisher Ron Middlebrook sitting next to Howards wife. Can you spot Lee Ritenour?

Right, This is the Gibson edition of the same model. Take note of how the sound hole dimensions have been modified slightly to accommodate the larger and heavier Gibson pickup, Note also the updated bridge and tailpiece, and the redesigned pickguard

This is an example of the original pre-merger Epiphone Howard Roberts.

thanks to GuitarPoint and Simon Gauff

Stratosphere

The guitar manufacturing industry was going through a boom time in the early '50s, experiencing a tidal wave of growth never seen before, or indeed since. Many companies that had been established since the pre war years, such as Harmony, Gibson, and Epiphone were, by the 1950s, churning out truckloads of the newly popular solid body electric guitars. They were quick and easy to produce, and comparatively cheap to buy too when compared to more traditional archtops. Although by no means the first one on the bus there is little doubt that Leo Fender was the flag bearer for this revolution when his Broadcaster appeared in 1950 followed by the Stratocaster in '54. Those perfect designs, along with Gibson's 1952 Les Paul, are very much still with us today. There were inevitably other brands who didn't have the market penetration or the financial resources of Fender or Gibson, and despite their quality and inventiveness, just didn't hang around for very long. One such marque was Stratosphere. This company was founded in Springfield Missouri by two brothers Russell and Claude Deaver. House painters by trade but with a great enthusiasm for music they started to manufacture guitars in 1954, but as it transpired not for very long as the company was wound up just four years later in 1958. Nobody knows exactly how many guitars were made during that period but most sources estimate a number close to 200. Most of you reading this may never have seen one, I certainly haven't, but as with many things their rarity has resulted in very high asking prices in the collector's market. Stratosphere made six string guitars, twelve string guitars, and 6/12 twin necks. No basses were made as far as I am aware. The body shape could best be described as a squashed up Les Paul Junior. The necks followed a Fender pattern, being screwed on through a mounting plate, and having maple fretboards. The individual guitars had a six-a-side headstock, the twin neck had a single side headstock on the six string side and of course a double sided headstock on the 12 string side. Rather unusually both of the twin neck heads were slotted. Also, unusually they were fitted with aluminum top nuts made in house by the Deavers themselves, as were most of the other component parts. Pickup type and configuration again generally followed the Fender model, though the control layout was totally different. Sunburst appears to have been the standard finish offering, but I have seen a photo of a blond guitar, and a red example, so possibly other finishes might have been available, unless of course that red one was the recipient of a much later respray. The biggest market for these guitars in the early '50s would have been the country market, rock and roll proper having yet to build up a head of steam, and the C&W scene was particularly strong in that part of the country. Luminaries such as Jimmy Bryant and Speedy West used Stratospheres regularly at that time, even being featured in the advertising material. As I said, I've never seen or played one of these, but they appear to be perfectly usable and playable guitars, quite attractive too, so they deserve their place in history, and it's a great pity that their lifespan was so brief. Russell Deaver died in 2009 aged 94.

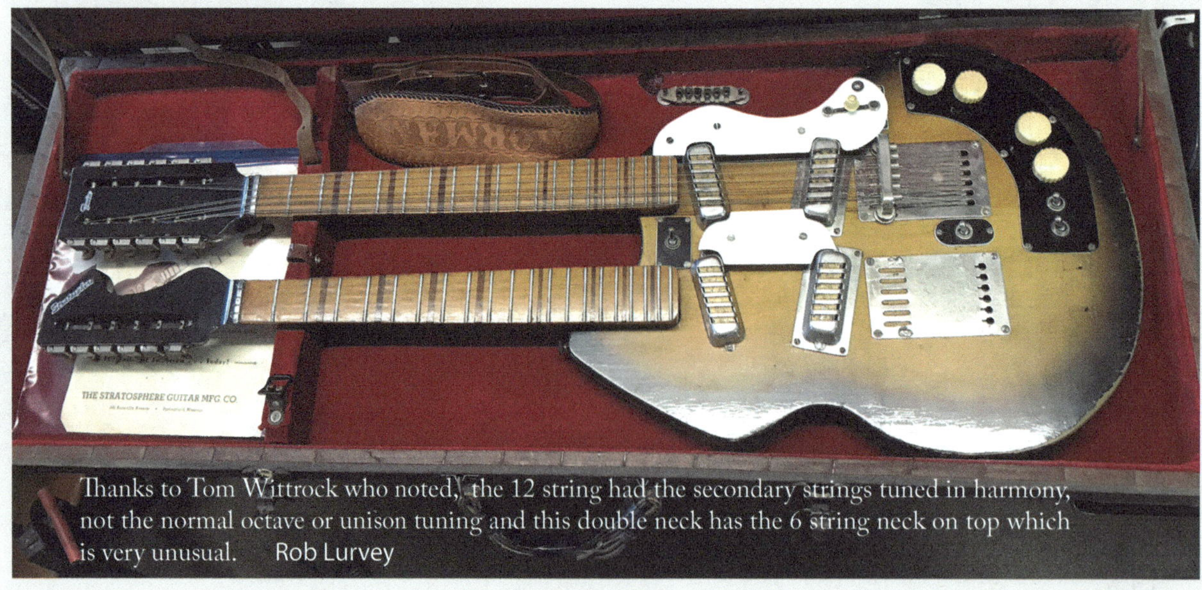

Thanks to Tom Wittrock who noted, the 12 string had the secondary strings tuned in harmony, not the normal octave or unison tuning and this double neck has the 6 string neck on top which is very unusual. Rob Lurvey

The **STRATOSPHERE** Guitar

Excitingly New! *Astonishingly* Different!

The Latest, Most *Revolutionary* Development in the Guitar World

The Guitar of Tomorrow . . . Today!

Played and recommended by Jimmy Bryant, West Coast television and Capitol recording star. Hear the "Stratosphere Boogie."

Also used by Chet Atkins on RCA Victor record "Somebody Stole My Gal" and others.

Write for full details

The Stratosphere Guitar Mfg. Co.

341 Boonville **Springfield, Missouri**

thanks to Rob Lurvey who has this fine example hanging in the reception area of his private collection in Springfield MO

TRAVIS BEAN GUITARS

Travis Bean

Innovation is an idea that creates value. What a great quote that is (I must confess it's not mine) and I can't think of a better fit than Travis Bean. A luthier and machinist, he began building guitars in 1974. His business partners were Gary Kramer and Marc McElwee, though Kramer departed after about a year to start up his own company, but more about that a little later. The guitars, and basses, were made to what was then a unique design format. The use of aluminum in guitar construction was nothing new but the way Bean merged together different construction techniques certainly was. As described elsewhere in these pages the Koa body of the guitar encased a milled billet of aluminum upon which were attached all component parts. The fretboard unusually was flat, requiring a slight adaptation of one's normal technique on a cambered fretboard, although later examples did feature a cambered fretboard, albeit with a very large radius camber. The extraordinary tapping technique employed by Stanley Jordan made good use of this feature. Around 3600 instruments were produced between 1974 and 1979 at which time the company ceased trading. There was a brief revival in the 1990s when a limited run of just 24 guitars were produced. Travis Bean died in 2011 aged just 63. Regrets, I've had a few, but selling my own Travis Bean back in the late '70s is right up there with the deepest of them.

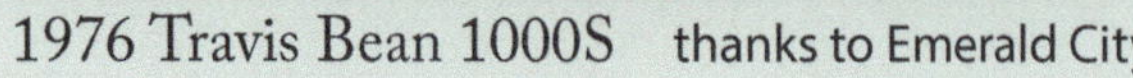

1976 Travis Bean 1000S thanks to Emerald City

This Koa wood TB was made for the 1977 world tour for ELP and featured on the song Karn Evil 9. With custom features for Greg Lake, two extra switches, a kill switch and a capacitor tone switch for the single coil sound.

Ned Steinberger had a vision, which, depending on your point of view, was a stroke of genius. Why do you need all of that weighty mass of a body, he reasoned, it contributes little to the sound or ergonomics of a guitar, so get rid of it. And why do the tuning keys have to be on a headstock, more length, and unnecessary weight. Let's fit them at the other end of the guitar, behind the bridge. So the Steinberger was conceived, and furthermore, made of plastic rather than wood, though his 'plastic' is correctly defined as being a graphite reinforced epoxy resin. What he came up with was little more than a stick with strings, although that sounds derogatory and I don't mean it to be, In theory, it's a really great idea, a totally groundbreaking approach to guitar design, and such leaps of faith are exactly what the industry needs, as without them we'd have no electric guitars at all. His first prototypes were made in 1977, and by 1979 he was producing instruments for retail sale. His first instruments were all basses, and no six string guitars were made until 1982. His guitars featured a patented Trans Trem system which is a little difficult to describe in brief here, but basically, it kept the strings in tune regardless of the movement of the tremolo (actually vibrato) and gave a player the ability to change the string tuning, and hence the key in which he or she was playing. Player's responses to these unusual guitars were mixed, you either loved them or hated them. I have played a couple, and they do feel very odd to anyone used to playing conventional guitars for many years. So, although they had their adherents, and still have, they could hardly be said to have set the world on fire. Various versions were made through the '80s, with differing pickup options for example. Genesis guitarist Mike Rutherford owned a Steinberger. He loved the way it played, and the way it sounded, but hated the way it looked. Legendary British luthier Roger Giffin was contacted to come up with an alternative. He broke the Steinberger down into parts and then fitted those parts to a more conventional wood body which he had constructed himself by hand. He gave the completed guitar back to Rutherford. "Perfect", he said. In due course, Ned Steinberger heard about this, eventually got to see Roger's modification, and was delighted. He told Roger that he had been experimenting with such bodies for a while but had never found a satisfactory answer. Roger's design became the M series. Steinberger sold out to Gibson in 1987. No guitars or basses were produced for some while following that date, but public demand has prompted Gibson to manufacture them again, although these are currently manufactured in South Korea. All being taken into account however, I consider the Steinberger instruments to be unique, and a positive contribution to the evolution of the electric guitar. The idea inspired other makers to reproduce or improve upon the basic premise and assimilate the idea into their own creations. One notable example is the broadly similar Erlewine Lazer, much favoured by the late great Johnny Winter.

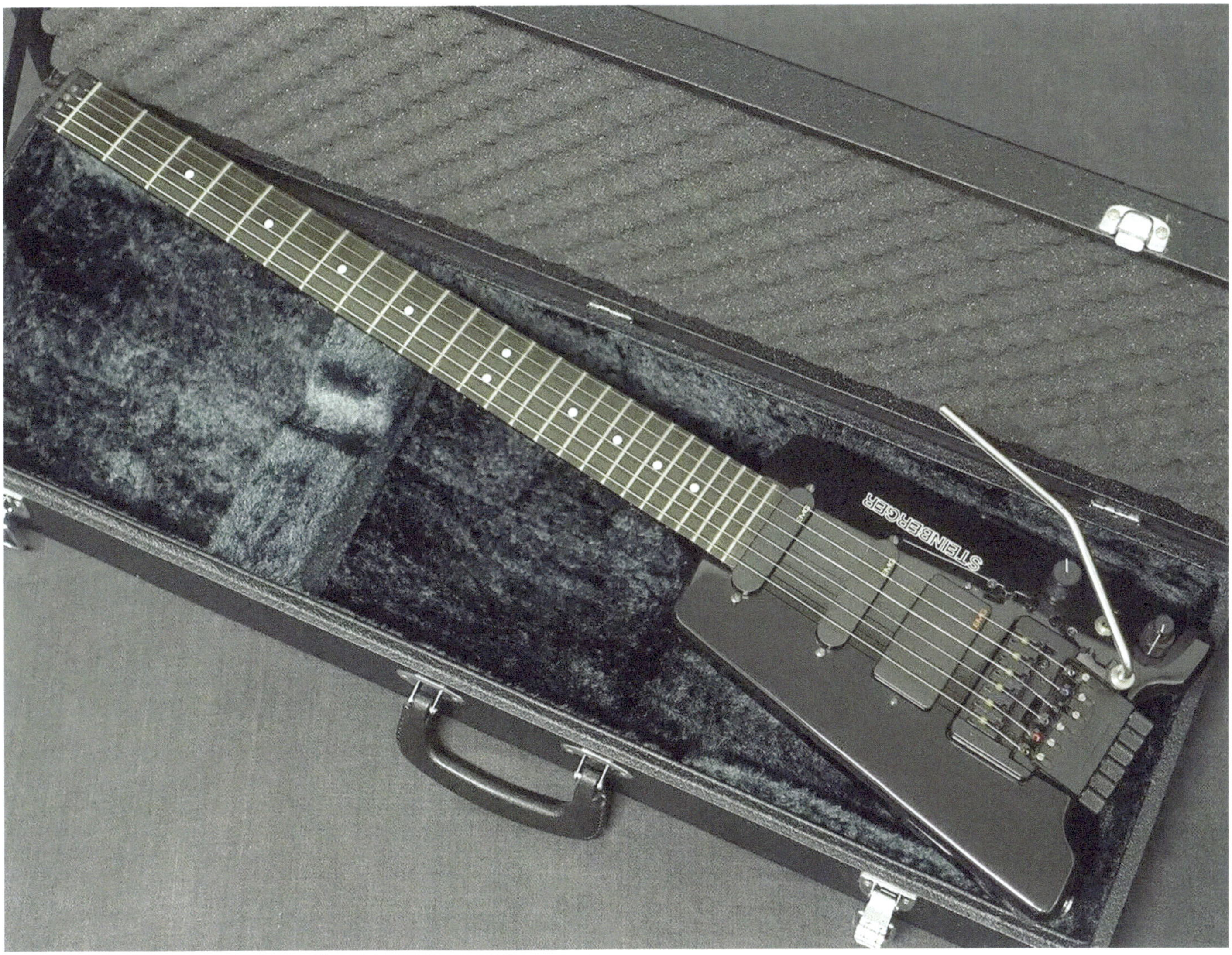

thanks to Sound Store - Japan

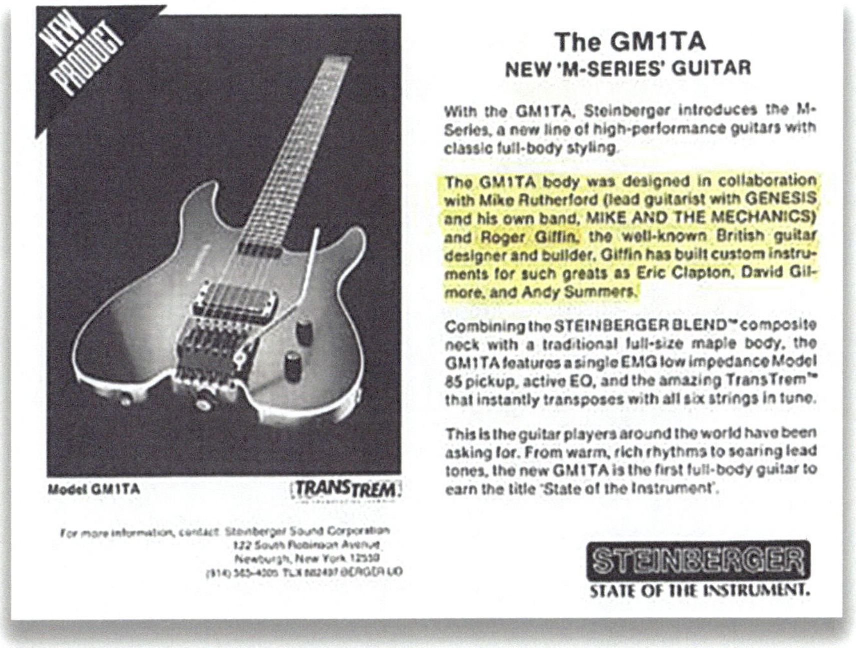

NEW PRODUCT

Model GM1TA

TRANSTREM

The GM1TA

NEW 'M-SERIES' GUITAR

With the GM1TA, Steinberger introduces the M-Series, a new line of high-performance guitars with classic full-body styling.

The GM1TA body was designed in collaboration with Mike Rutherford (lead guitarist with GENESIS and his own band, MIKE AND THE MECHANICS) and Roger Giffin, the well-known British guitar designer and builder. Giffin has built custom instruments for such greats as Eric Clapton, David Gilmore, and Andy Summers.

Combining the STEINBERGER BLEND™ composite neck with a traditional full-size maple body, the GM1TA features a single EMG low impedance Model 85 pickup, active EQ, and the amazing TransTrem™ that instantly transposes with all six strings in tune.

This is the guitar players around the world have been asking for. From warm, rich rhythms to searing lead tones, the new GM1TA is the first full-body guitar to earn the title 'State of the Instrument'.

For more information, contact: Steinberger Sound Corporation
122 South Robinson Avenue
Newburgh, New York 12550
(914) 565-4005 TLX 882497 BERGER UD

STATE OF THE INSTRUMENT.

How Fender joined the Thinline boom

Exactly in the same way that Gibson had concerns about losing solid body sales to Fender, over in California Fender became painfully aware of the fact that a major potential part of their market, the semi acoustic guitar, was being dominated by Gibson, Epiphone, and others, like the Guild Starfire range, also Gretsch models such as the Tennessean and Country Club. They wanted a slice of that lucrative market. This change in direction was generated in the main by the early '60s British invasion. All of a sudden there were all of these British bands on the Ed Sullivan show, like the Beatles, The Animals, Herman's Hermits and the rest, all of whom were sporting Gretsch Tennesseans or Epiphone Casinos and Rivoli basses. The writing was on the wall. The first semi-acoustic guitar they came up with was the Fender Coronado, released in 1966. This was designed by Roger Rossmeisl (remember him?) and was a thin hollow body guitar, with double cutaway following the Gibson/Epiphone pattern. The model range was made up of a single pickup version, a twin pickup, a twelve string, and two basses, one a single pickup and one a double. Following Fender's habit, they each had a bolt on neck. All were equipped, unusually, with DeArmond pickups. They were offered in sunburst finish as standard, and a wide variety of custom colours, including the spectacular Wildwood models, which were made from timbers streaked with one of six colours, an effect which was achieved by injecting trees with coloured dye as they grew, a process which took three years. The Coronado model was discontinued in 1972, and, it has to be said, never really hit the mark. Nonetheless, they were reissued in 2013, though this time they had a body with an anti feedback block running through the body, like Gibson's ES335, and featured upgraded pickups. Their next foray into semi acoustics was the Starcaster, launched in 1976. Unlike the symmetry of the Coronado, this one featured an offset-contour body with a unique reversed headstock. They were still hollow bodied and with the same bolt on neck construction. They never really hit the mark either and were discontinued in either 1980 or 1982 depending on who you believe. In common with the Coronado, they were briefly reissued in 2013, and a Starcaster guitar now forms part of Fender's budget Squier range.

Once again, we are indebted to Rob Lurvey and his amazing collection. These stunning photos show Rob's fascination with the Coronado model which features most of the available colours. With guitars, 12 string, bass guitars, and the exotic Wildwoods, he has made a lifetime work of seeking out the best available examples.

FENDER LTD

Not content with attempting to grab a portion of the thin body semi market they also turned their attention to full bodied arch top jazz guitars. Back to Roger Rossmeisl once more, who designed two full bodied jazz guitars that were ready to go on sale in 1968. The first was the LTD. Many thousands had been spent on the R&D required, and the workshop machinery, to even make this guitar a reality, and it was the most expensive guitar ever made by Fender at that point. Like Gibson's prime models it had a carved top and back and was fitted with a floating pickup to allow the top to resonate effectively. It proved to be expensive and time consuming to produce, and the whole project was shelved after a mere 36 examples had been made. Needless to say, the experiment cost Fender, owned by CBS at the time, a lot of money. Roger Rossmeisl's other jazz guitar project was the Montego, again a full bodied jazz guitar, and also released in 1968. The bodies were made in Germany and shipped to California in a finished condition, simply requiring final assembly which included fixing the neck, and either one or two humbuckers depending on the model. These were cheaper than the LTD, though still pretty expensive compared to Telecasters, etc. The Montego, never a big seller, was discontinued in 1973. They were nice looking guitars, and well made, but there were issues. One was the high price. Another was the fact that players had always associated Fender with building solid bodies and a Fender jazz guitar was just a step too far, but probably the most crucial issue, which led to their downfall, was the bolt on neck. Traditional jazz players were never going to accept that. All told a very expensive mistake. In 1999 Fender entered into a licensing agreement with ace arch top maker Bob Benedetto. The plan was to build high quality full bodied guitars in Fender's Custom shop facility. The guitars that were produced are described by the cognoscenti as Fenderettos. The agreement ended in 2006. It isn't clear how many were eventually produced but I'm sure the numbers are likely to be in the low hundreds rather than thousands. Fender has not produced any further full bodied guitars in the years since.

ALEMBIC GUITARS

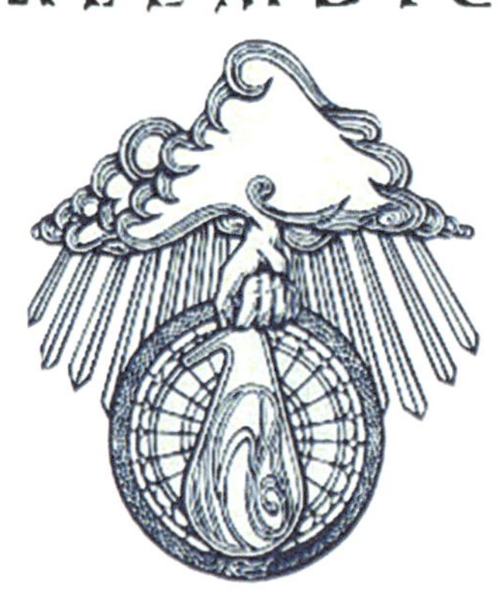

The next maker I want to turn my attention to couldn't be more different. The genesis of the Alembic company was almost solely due to Augustus' Stanley Owsley III, yes, THAT Augustus' Stanley Owsley III who, in addition to his undeniable skills in creating recreational pharmaceuticals, was a gifted electronics and sound engineer. He had a workshop borrowed from the Grateful Dead, in which he designed and built the Dead's Wall Of Sound touring rig, which at its peak weighed in at nine and a half tons. His workshop, and his newer recording facility, were named Pacific High Recording Studios. By 1969 he had joined forces with Ron and Susan Wickersham, Bob Matthews, all of whom had backgrounds in sound engineering or recording, and guitarist turned luthier Rick Turner. They collectively decided to rename their new company Alembic. Their mission was to improve the quality of the band's live sound reinforcement equipment, and the quality of their live recordings, a subject especially important at that time to the Dead. As far as guitars were concerned, they, and Ron Wickersham especially, started down that road by modifying and improving the guitars and basses of David Crosby, Jerry Garcia, and Jefferson Airplane's Jack Casady amongst many others of the Bay Area glitterati. One thing that Ron had in common with Les Paul was a firm belief in the benefits of low impedance pickups which he regularly retrofitted to modify existing guitars and basses. The very first Alembic branded bass guitar was made for Casady in 1972, followed a year later by another for bass phenomenon Stanley Clarke. All Alembic basses, and guitars, are built with low imp pickups, and on-board active electronics. Almost all feature a well established neck through construction. Very rarely, if ever, will you see a guitar made with the same high degree of craftsmanship that you see on an Alembic. The bodies are produced from rarely seen timbers such as Zebrawood, Bubinga, Purple Heart wood, and bird's-eye maple, all sandwiched together in a variety of ways, with no two instruments being exactly the same. Production in significant numbers began in '73, basses considerably outselling six strings, and the Who's John Entwistle soon became a devotee. I've been looking through scores of old photos of him and have identified four distinctly different basses that he owned, and there might well have been others. Mark King of Level 42 also uses one to great effect. Alembic instruments aren't cheap, but despite of the price tags production numbers have steadily increased over those past fifty or so years. The current catalogue features nine bass models and eight guitars, all of which have prices that run into five figures. They, naturally enough, will also produce custom made one-offs to order. Currently, around 1500 guitars and basses leave their Santa Rosa facility every year. The factory employs eleven craftspeople, all of whom are either members of the extended Wickersham family or are close friends. Augustus Owsley Stanley III died in a car accident in Queensland Australia in 2011, though many years had passed since he last had any direct association with Alembic

1976 Alembic Series 1

thanks to Frank Manno

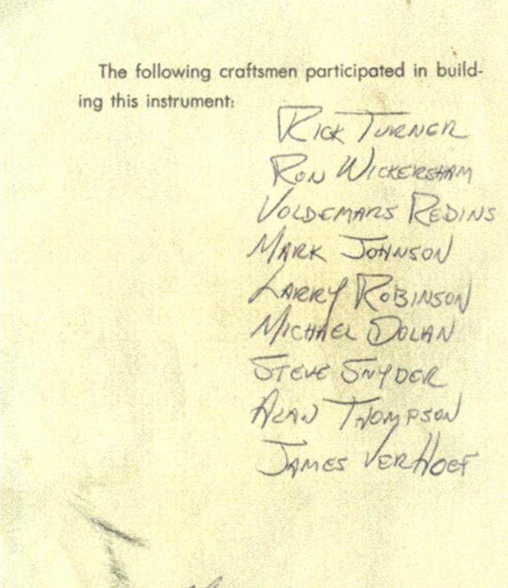

The following craftsmen participated in building this instrument:

Rick Turner
Ron Wickersham
Voldemars Redins
Mark Johnson
Larry Robinson
Michael Dolan
Steve Snyder
Alan Thompson
James VerHoef

Date: May 21 1976

ALEMBIC

Model: Long Scale Bass

Serial # USA AF 76 410

A Long Scale Bass, it was designed and built by a team that included Rick Turner, it had a laminated body with mahogany at its core, and a neck of maple and amaranth (purpleheart). With active electronics it has different settings and there were supplementary switches by each tone control. Played on countless sessions at Muscle Shoals.

Today, it remains in all-original condition, and Manno loves how smoothly it plays. "You can coax a variety of tones from it," he said. "It's very comfortable, and even at 11 pounds, it doesn't feel too heavy.

AMPEG

All of that leads me very neatly to Ampeg, whose importance is often overlooked. The Ampeg brand name derives from Amplified Peg. No, not a member of Grateful Dead's entourage but a transducer related device fitted inside a wooden peg that was intended to fit into a hole in the lower part of the body of an upright string bass. A simple thing, and in principle still with us today, though much improved in design and efficiency. These were first made in 1948 and resolved the quandary that bass players had of not being heard over the blast from big bands, exactly the same complaint that guitarists had been wittering on about for years. They had moderate success with the device but Ampeg felt that they could take this further, and in 1961 or 1962, sources vary, so they came out with the Baby Bass. Still an upright and fretless bass, it had a much reduced body dimension, actually more the size of a small cello, and was made of plastic. This, it was hoped, would appeal across the board, to big bands, whose popularity was declining by this time anyway, to rock n roll and pop groups, and to jazz trios and quartets. It never really took off, and the growing prominence of the bass guitar sounded their death knell. The first Ampeg bass guitar, the AUB-1 appeared in 1967, and what a monster it was, with quite a large and heavy body, and with f-holes that were cut right through the body. The neck was almost as if it had been grafted on from an upright classical style bass, still with the violin curved headstock. First run models were fretless, though fretted versions soon appeared, along with a couple of model variations, and those same early versions also had a transducer fitted inside the body, not visible externally. Later versions of the bass were fitted with conventional electromagnetic pickups which improved tone and volume dramatically. I really feel that I can't leave the subject of Ampeg without referring to their amplifiers. As the craze for electric guitars snowballed through the '50s and '60s the Ampeg company saw a chance to sell amplification to all of those two guitar, bass, and drum groups. After all, they had plenty of experience. They came up with a series of both guitar and bass combos, all covered in a smart dark blue textured vinyl. One was the Reverbrocket introduced in the early '60s, which claimed to be the first amp to have a built in reverb, though I know there are those who will hotly dispute that. Next was the Portaflex intended for bass. It had a very clever feature, the amplifier itself was stored upside down inside the cabinet during transport and was to be lifted out and turned upright during use. Brilliant. Ampeg though is best known for their monster 300 watt SVT amps and cabinets, their sheer power even eclipsing that of Marshall. Popular with the Rolling Stones who used them exclusively for decades, and with any other band who wanted to make a lot of noise.

Ampeg AUB-1 Electric Bass Guitar (1967) Ampeg AUSB-1 Electric Bass Guitar (1967)

thanks to Retrofret for these imges

1966 Ampeg AEB-1 Bass
Black with white guard # 090 1st issue

Dan Armstrong

Dan Armstrong was a guitarist and luthier, and highly skilled at both. In the late '60s he was employed by Ampeg on a consultancy basis, and he offered to them his ideas for a revolutionary new guitar to be manufactured under the Ampeg brand. What he came up with was certainly something new. The body was moulded from a clear plexiglass, often referred to as lucite. The wood effect pickguards had Ampeg Dan Armstrong printed on them. It had a bolt on neck, and was supplied with two pickups, made by Bill Lawrence, which slotted into a cavity close to the bridge. One was wound in a way that gave it a bassy rhythm response, and the other a more trebly tone, intended for lead guitar parts. These could be swapped quickly and easily. The guitars were launched in 1968. In truth they weren't the first ever plastic guitars, the Italian Eko company were making such things in the early '60s, and, as we know, many lapsteels, even pre war examples, were made from bakelite and other plastics. It was rumoured that the first Gibson Les Paul solid bodies were to have been made of plastic too, but that never transpired, thankfully. The idea of interchangeable pickups however was new. Although the guitars were never made in vast numbers they were, somewhat surprisingly perhaps, quite well received. Keith Richards was very fond of his and used it extensively. A Japanese maker, and I forget who, reissued the guitar in 1998. Around 1970 or so Dan cut his ties with Ampeg and moved to London. During the '70s I was working in a guitar shop in London's Denmark Street, centre of the guitar retail trade, and Dan became a regular, and very welcome customer. I recall one occasion when we bought from him a Gibson Les Paul Special that had been stripped back to the wood. Shortly thereafter we sold it on to Marc Bolan, but he returned it within a few days as he really wanted a guitar with humbuckers. I eventually sold that same guitar on to Bob Marley. It became closely associated with him and he used it for his entire career. But I digress. Once in London, it wasn't too long before Dan resumed his passion for building guitars, and he came up with a new Dan Armstrong model. Rather than plastic the new one was mahogany, and somewhat close in proportions to his Ampeg original, still with a bolt on neck. He'd extended his range now to include a six string guitar, a short scale bass, and a long scale bass. No interchangeable pickups this time, but just one that slid from end to end on a metal rail fixed to the body. A good idea in theory, and surprising in a way that nobody had thought of it before, not as far as I'm aware anyway. Years later Gibson made a bass with a sliding pickup, but despite the obvious benefit of such a thing no other makers have taken up the idea. Dan Armstrong was a true innovator with some unique ideas. That DNA has filtered down to his son Kent Armstrong who makes some of the best pickups in the world.

thanks toMusicians Headquarters Texas

thanks to Sound Store Japan

BURNS GUITARS

A more successful UK guitar maker was James Ormston Burns, known to all as Jimmy. He started making guitars in 1959, and guitars bearing the Burns brand are still being made to this day, although Jimmy himself is long gone. The first guitar to bear his name was a simple and rather primitive looking solid body but he soon got into his stride and was producing models such as the Vista Sonic, Shortscale Jazz, and the awesome Bison, and it's sister Bison Bass, at the time the most expensive UK made guitars to be marketed, more expensive in fact than some well known American imports. A series of transistor amplifiers such as the Orbit 40, and Orbit 60, were also made during this period. The Burns company struggled financially, basically due to mis-management, the result being that Burns was bought out by American giant Baldwin in 1965. It might be of interest to some that US imports of Burns guitars were carried out by Ampeg until the Baldwin takeover. Jimmy himself remained as chief designer, although the pickguards of his guitars now bore the name Baldwin instead of his.

Always a tinkerer he came up with the oddly designed Steer. Bandit, Magpie, and Scorpion models. They weren't around for long. Even more odd, for it's time anyway, was the Flyte, a carved arrow shaped body finished in silver with a bolt on neck. Jimmy had some great ideas but they didn't always stick. He also made a round hole flat top guitar with two pickups called a Virginian. They ran from 1965 to 1968 but comparatively few were made. In my opinion, one of his most successful experiments was the TR2. This was a double cutaway slim bodied guitar, rather following the ethos of Gibson's 335. The controls were either fitted to the top surface of the pickguard or were pinwheel controls that poked out from the underside depending upon the batch. The most memorable feature of the TR2's however is that they were the first ever electric guitars with on-board active electronics and had a transistor preamp installed under the pickguard. These were expensive to make and were only in the catalogue for one year, 1963. Arguably, however, the most instantly recognisable and memorable Burns guitar was the Hank Marvin Shadows model, with a matching bass. These were made for the Shadows and were good enough to cause Hank and Co to ditch their Fenders, for a while at least. Financial turbulence persisted within the company, but eventually, Jim Burns did regain control of his company and his name. There followed a flurry of new models, but the Burns that we knew and loved was history. So briefly the Korean made Burns Club series were introduced in 1999 in reality nothing more than a Fender Stratocaster copy with Burns written on it, and the Chinese made Cobra series a little later, and that's where we are. Jimmy Burns was a very clever and intuitive guitar designer and builder, and was solely responsible for introducing significant innovations to the UK guitar industry, though some seemed pretty off-the-wall at the time. Without him, however, things would have been a lot different, and we would have been the poorer for that.

Burns TR-2   thanks to Walt Grace Vintage

HAYMAN

SHERGOLD

Despite the dominance in the UK market of the Big Six American makers, particularly at the top end, and the overwhelming quantity of Japanese made guitars supplying the lower end, there were some British made guitars edging their way in as well. They occupied a mid market position in the overall scheme of things, and many British players will have cut their teeth on guitars made by Burns, Grimshaw, or Watkins, which are mentioned elsewhere in these pages, much in the same way as our American friends might have started their careers on a Harmony or Kay. In East London in the late 1960s there existed a woodworking shop owned by Jack Golder and Norman Houlder, both of whom were ex Burns employees. By this time they were building bespoke items of furniture but their woodworking skills also still extended to making guitar bodies which were sold on to manufacturers such as Rosetti, Burns, and well known UK musical wholesalers Barnes And Mullins. In 1969 they hooked up anew with Jim Burns and ex Vox employee Bob Pearson and this team began building a range of guitars bearing the brand name Hayman. The Hayman brand was owned by Dallas Arbiter, which also included a line of drums, and it was the Dallas group which were to promote and market Hayman guitars. The instruments themselves were well made and were touted in their own advertising blurb as being the Finest Guitars In The World. Good, they may have been, but that was a bit of a stretch. The slab bodies were quite Telecaster-ish but with a deeper left side cutaway, the strings pulled through from the back, another very Telecaster-ish feature. The maple necks were super-slim with a six a side headstock which was very obviously a Jim Burns design. There were double pickup models, a three pickup version, and a bass. Jim Burns departed in 1971 to concentrate on his own projects. Incidentally between '71 and '74 they also manufactured a separate line of guitars under the Ned Callan brand. The Haymans were good guitars and I can remember selling scores of them. There was however bad news on the horizon when the Dallas Arbiter group folded in 1974. Now down to a three man team following the departure of Burns, and with no distributor or marketing, Bob Pearson decided nonetheless to push on, using a new brand name Shergold.

to be continued

Original Hayman advertising material showing the '1010' model, with '2020' inset.

1974 Hayman 3030 H
as made famous by Graham Coxon

HAYMAN

SHERGOLD

The Shergold brand was launched in 1975 and initially was made from the existing stock of leftover Hayman parts. The Shergold range was broadly similar to the Haymans, but now included a 6/12 twin neck and a separate 12 string model. There was also a rather interesting variation called The Modulator, which featured a control panel that could be quickly unclipped and replaced with another with different tone circuitry. A good idea and I'm quietly surprised that other manufacturers didn't take it up. Their most popular model was the Masquerader and the same model still retains a place in the current Shergold range, albeit with a slightly modified body outline. According to industry figures, In purely numerical terms, the UK guitar market peaked in 1977, and from then on sales throughout the industry steadily declined, or at best remained stubbornly static, and the popular music scene of the '80s became dominated by synth-pop, rap, techno, and house music, for which, sadly, guitars were not required. Unable to ride out this crisis, Shergold collapsed in 1982. The team soldiered on, making furniture once more, plus the occasional guitar to custom order. There was a Shergold re-launch in 1992 which met with limited success, and Jack Golder also passed away in 1992 which must have resulted in a considerable loss of momentum for the Shergold brand. In 2015 the brand was purchased by the aforementioned Barnes and Mullins, and Shergold enjoyed another re-launch in 2017. The format of the new generation of Shergolds was overseen by noted UK luthier Patrick James Eggle, who was also a major shareholder. Eggle is also responsible for the Faith guitar brand, in addition to making his own eponymous guitar line. No longer are Shergold a domestic British brand, however, as they are now produced in China or Indonesia.

MASQUERADER

PROVOCATEUR

Masqueraders started with serial number 3101 on 8th Nov '75, making this the 10th example built. The first 250 or so Masqueraders featured re-badged Hayman necks with the more ornate curvy headstock outline and decorative rebates on the sides. Also usually featuring a hole where the Hayman logo was to have been fitted
thanks to Black Guitars

The first Shergold Masquerader. The extremely rare guitar was found in an attic in Milford Haven, Wales.
Thanks to Music Instrument News

PATRICK JAMES EGGLE

There are many instances described within these pages of one-off custom builders who have gone on to make the transition to full production mode ultimately employing teams of skilled craftsmen and investing capital in significant workshop facilities. In general, this is owing to the reputation of the founder, and of the fine quality of instruments he made. Patrick James Eggle is one member of this exclusive club. He began making guitars in the early 1990s, and his Berlin model was first offered, on a limited basis, in 1991. This was a carved top solid with an asymmetrical body, in fact not unlike a PRS to look at. These were well liked by guitar players everywhere, even though availability was limited. The supply conundrum was solved by Eggle employing more staff and expanding his operation. His original workshop was in Coventry, later moved to Birmingham, and finally to a much bigger facility in Oswestry, Shropshire where he remains to this day. In 1992 he founded Patrick James Eggle Guitars Ltd, and by the mid '90s, his factory was producing around 2000 guitars a year. Quite a leap in such a short time. Eggle moved to the US in 1994 but returned to the UK in 2004. Production continued in his absence. Aside from his own Eggle branded guitars he also designed the Faith series of Asian made acoustics. Eggle made acoustics too, but production of all acoustics ceased in 2016 so he could concentrate his efforts on his solid electrics. In 2017, in association with UK wholesaler Barnes And Mullins, he assisted in the relaunch of the Shergold brand, coming up with a new design for the Masquerader model. By this time the Eggle Berlin model had been discontinued and Eggle had launched a new range, all having a fairly conservative look. There were, and are, three base models, a single cutaway solid, a T-type, and an S-type, though this version had a warmed over body design which was slightly smaller and lighter. There are a large number of variations currently available on those three models, in addition to which Eggle maintain their own Custom Shop where you can order virtually anything you want. All Eggles are built in the UK to uncompromising standards and therefore don't come cheap. At time of writing the majority of models list at between £4000 and £5000. Nothing new or innovative here, just another gold star for entrepreneurship, and world class instruments that contribute another quality brand to the current market, and they're not Chinese.

Oz series

Graham Coxon

Macon Green Burst

SUHR

John Suhr, a guitar player, and enthusiast, began building his guitars in 1974 and produced the first Suhr branded example in 1984 at his workshop in New York. In 1991 he moved to Los Angeles and continued his work, building guitars to very high-end specifications. Between 1995 and 1997 he worked at Fender's Custom Shop, and in '97 formed his own established company. His current range of guitars follows familiar Fender outlines, and he is offering Stratocaster, Telecaster and Jazzmaster style guitars, but made his way. He also has the Aura model in the catalogue, based on a Les Paul design. He also manufactures his own pickups and prides himself on the fact that all his guitars are hand wired, and neck profiles can be tailored to an individual player's requirements. A range of hand wired Suhr amplifiers complement the range, and bass guitars too.

Pete Thorn is an endorsee of Suhr products performing regular workshops and shows with the Classic Rock Band plus YouTube blogs.

Heritage Guitar Inc.

In 1985 the Gibson company, which had been established at 225 Parsons Street, Kalamazoo, Michigan for the best part of a century, decided to up sticks and move to Nashville. Not all staff wished to relocate, and as all of the production machinery was to remain in situ, so did they. The remaining staff under a new banner continued making guitars as they always had, same machinery, same people, same methods, same coffee machine. No longer able to use the Gibson name they came up with the brand Heritage, reflecting the long and auspicious history of the Parsons Street location. Production in Kalamazoo continues, and their current catalog features well known classics. There's a Les Paul lookalike, a 335 lookalike, a 175 lookalike, and so on. They also have a custom shop where one-offs can be built to order. If you asked them, I'm sure that they would quietly say, with due deference to Gibson of course, that Heritage guitars are what Gibson's would be like now, had they not moved. Incidentally, they now share their factory floor with the current incarnation of the Harmony company.

1989 Heritage H-150 - note the original Les Paul shape

courtesy, Heritage Guitars

PEAVEY

As most of you probably know Hartley Peavey, a one time amplifier repairman based in Meridian Mississippi decided to start up his own amplifier production facility in the mid '60s. This enterprise became successful, and by the late '70s and into the '80s Peavey had become the largest amp manufacturer in the world, eclipsing even the all conquering Marshall. At some point in the mid '70s he decided to expand into making guitars, and his first, the T60 was launched in 1977, along with its sister T40 bass, and was in the catalogue for a further ten years or thereabouts. It was a natural finish double cutaway body, though other finishes later became available. Nothing exceptional to look at but it was a start. To give Hartley due credit it did incorporate some interesting features, including interesting pickup switching options, and was made using what were then very up to date production methods, CNC machines, and the like, common everywhere today. His highly efficient and economical production methods resulted in an American made guitar that was at the time selling at around one third of the price of a Fender Stratocaster. Many other models followed, including the budget priced Raptor series, a jazz style deep semi called the Rockingham, and a slew of other solids, too many to describe here, most of which were ultimately made in South Korea or Vietnam. Due to a combination of several factors, which included over expansion, (he had up to seven factories operating simultaneously), over capitalisation on stock and equipment, a steadily shrinking and over saturated market, the financial crash of 2008, and inefficient management, revealed by one of those Undercover Boss TV shows, the timing of which was unfortunate, a perfect storm, and thus his company inevitably collapsed. The Peavey name is now owned by a Chinese company and evidently has been since the twenty-teens. New amp models, and new guitar models are being launched as I write this, along tried and tested lines no doubt.

Tone House

Killer vintage

Music Man

In 1971, ex Fender vice president, Forrest White, together with Tom Walker, and recruiting Leo Fender, initially as a sleeping partner but eventually company president, formed an amplifier manufacturing company, which, after a couple of initial name changes, finally became Musicman. Their first amp was the excellent HD65 which utilized a combination of solid state technology and traditional valve circuitry. However, it is their guitars that interest us here. Their plans to introduce a line of instruments were complete by 1976 and in that year they introduced the Stingray six string guitar and Stingray bass. Nothing new to look at, and the Fender influence sat heavily on their shoulders. The one and only distinctive difference was the configuration of the machine heads. Basses had three on the bass side, and one on the treble side, and guitars had four on the bass side and two on the treble. That unique format continues to this day. The bass however hit the market just at the right time, coinciding as it did with the craze for funk bass, and a rise in the acceptance of the bass as a solo instrument in its own right. For that reason, it sold very well. The guitar though was a bit "ho-hum" and simply didn't sell. In 1978 a two pickup Sabre bass was added to the range which continued until '84, by which time the Stingray guitar had been discontinued. It is probably fair to say that the company's performance during those early years was patchy, and thus it was that the company was sold to Ernie Ball in 1984.

MUSIC MAN AND STANDEL GUITARS

At the time Ernie Ball was dominant in the guitar string market, arguably the biggest selling string brand globally, even universally. You could probably buy his strings on the planet Zarg in the Andromeda Galaxy. This change of ownership, and its subsequent new direction, was exactly what the Musicman brand name needed. Production of the Stingray bass continued, and that of a Cutlass bass, which featured a graphite neck which Leo Fender is said to have hated. Their OLP budget line (officially licensed product) was built in the far east, from the late 1990s to 2008, and a later Sterling series, named for Ernie Ball's son, were made in Indonesia from 2009. Back in the US the SUB series were being made utilizing faster production methods, and, it has to be said, cheaper materials. Musicman makes attractive guitars, with a unique body design, and became the favoured axe of Albert Lee, hence their Albert Lee model, that of Steve Morse, and also that of Eddie Van Halen. After his acrimonious departure from Kramer, EVH hooked up with Musicman and together they designed a version to his specifications. These were launched in the early '90s and were made for five years. Once his endorsement agreement ended the same guitar continued to be on sale under the Axis name.

STANDEL

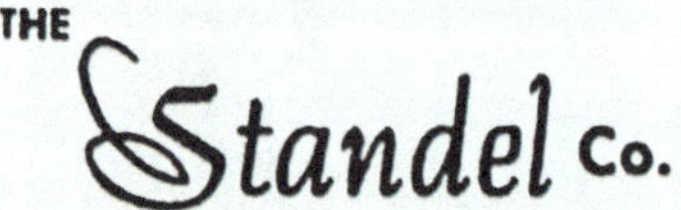

At time of writing Musicman continue. Standel were best known as an amplifier manufacturer, and had been since 1952. The company reasoned that if they made amps then why not make guitars to go with them. The very first guitars with the Standel brand were in reality rebranded Dobros and we're being sold under the Standel name from 1962. Standel's Bakersfield neighbours happened to be Mosrite, Seimie Moseley became involved, built ten prototypes for Standel, and between 1960 and around 1966 Standel solid electrics were in production, heavily influenced by the Mosrite design. It appears that a year or so later Standel guitars were made by the Harptone company and the new expanded range included some rather attractive single cutaway slimline semi acoustics, somewhat akin to an Epiphone Sorrento. Of particular note is the fact that the very first acoustic bass guitar was made by Harptone at this time and bore the Standel name. The Harptone association continued until 1969, and no Standel guitars were made after that time. For reasons I won't expand on here the Standel company experienced terminal financial problems and in 1971 was purchased by another amp company Randall. Around a year later they were purchased again by Gibson owners Norlin, but the company was finally wound up after about another year. Although their time in the sun was fairly brief they did produce some nice instruments. Never in vast quantities however, and it's quite likely that you've never seen one, but they do pop up on collectors sites once in a while. No more guitars, but the Standel name survives on a range of boutique amplifiers.

1960s Standel 910-S Sunburst - courtesy of Norm's Rare Guitars

The world of commerce can be unpredictable and often harsh. Most companies experience rough seas from time to time, it would be surprising if they didn't, and the guitar manufacturing industry is no exception. Most of the familiar names have gone through lean periods with a variety of final outcomes. Some of their misfortune can be laid at the door of market forces, aggressive competition, failure to keep abreast of the latest trends, and a variety of other factors. Sometimes the problems are of the company's own making. Choosing my words carefully to avoid litigation, no names here, there have been instances in the industry of poor planning, failure to address design, build quality, or component quality issues, or else just plain incompetence.

By 1969 Gibson was under the aegis of the Norlin group. It appears that they'd said to Gibson something along the lines of "Nice guitars guys, but just way too expensive". I wish I'd been a fly on the office wall during that meeting. The inevitable outcome was that Norlin embarked on a rigorous cost cutting exercise with a view to producing at least some guitars with markedly lower retail prices, and, at the same time, fight back against the tide of cheap Japanese imports. In this strategy of course, Gibson was not alone. At one level this would seem to be a perfectly sensible and logical approach, but, in my view, they went about it in the wrong way and ended up producing some of the poorest quality guitars bearing the Gibson brand ever to have been made.

The first range to go on the chopping block were the SGs. The Junior was dropped and entirely redesigned Specials, Standards and Customs appeared in 1971. The Special was renamed SG Professional, the SG Standard was renamed the SG Deluxe and the Custom was left as was. All three models featured a suspended Les Paul style pickguard and all controls were pre-installed on a D shaped escutcheon plate that just dropped into the body. Much cheaper and quicker to make than previous SGs had been. All three guitars were available in a rather nasty new walnut finish, the color of the stuff you'd use to paint your garden fence, though the Professional and Deluxe were also available in cherry. As it was to turn out these models didn't stick around for too long and by 1973 the headline SG range had reverted to more or less its pre-Norlin look, once again featuring a Custom, Standard, and Special. They now had controls fitted directly to the body, the early '60s "comma" style pickguards, and one major update being the small coil humbucking pickups now fitted to the Special. though with a black plastic cover rather than chrome. The Custom and the Standard now had the Schaller style bridge fitted which enabled a longer saddle travel. Still no Junior. Incidentally, a satin walnut finish became an available option on the Standard from 1974 and for the first time a tobacco sunburst finish from 1975. Cherry was an option post 1976. White finished Customs were available once again from 1974.

1971 SG-II
Cherry

1971SG-3

1974
ES150-TD Walnut

1974
Les-Paul Custom

GIBSON THE NORLIN YEARS

Despite Norlin's best intentions those '71 SGs were not well received and didn't sell well. I don't think any of you reading this would argue if I said they were ugly and looked cheap, rather like that forgettable blind date you once had. Things at Gibson couldn't get any worse, could they? Well yes, actually they could. Also in 1971, Norlin discontinued the entry level Melody Maker range, which would not reappear until the mid '70s, albeit in a different form with SG style bodies. The range was replaced by the SG100, SG200, and SG250. There were also a grand total of four basses, the SB100, SB200, SB300, and SB400. The guitars carried over the same single coil Melody Maker pickups, but they were now mounted into a chrome oval plate, the controls mounted also on a Telecaster style chrome plate set at an angle on the lower right hand side of the body. The SG100 had one pickup, the SG200 two, the SG250 being the same except with a cherry sunburst finish rather than the garden fence brown. The body sculpturing, or bevelling, was reduced substantially on these SGs compared to earlier '60s examples and they were a bit plank-like. These guitars had little, if any, aesthetic appeal and once, again, sales were less than encouraging. In a sense Norlin had achieved one objective, they now had guitars on sale, the prices of which were compatible with the Japanese opposition that they were trying so desperately to outflank. The only remaining factor was that if you put one of those SGs alongside a Japanese guitar on a shop wall, as I had to do daily, the Japanese guitar would invariably sell first. It looked more appealing and desirable, the finish was better, and was frankly simply more saleable. Things weren't exactly going well for Gibson in the early '70s. Things couldn't get any worse, could they? Well yes actually they could. That latest run of SGs sold poorly, were discontinued in 1973 and replaced by the SG1, SG2, and SG3. Again, very simple, basic, and cheap to make. They had the same raised scratchplates that the Deluxe and Professional had, and featured pickups much like the old Firebird pickups, humbucking but with no pole screws, but now with black plastic covers. The 1 and 2 were in cherry only and the 3 in cherry sunburst only. These at least were spared the fencing paint. Still not a great seller this line was discontinued in 1975, and at that point, Gibson very wisely chose to cease making ultra-cheap guitars and leave that task to the Japanese who could do it much better. This was to become academic anyway as Gibson were shortly to start producing their own Japanese guitars under the Epiphone banner.

Not to be overlooked were the popular series of thinline semi-acoustics, and it was to them that Norlin next directed their attention. Production of the ES335 ES345 and ES355 continued unabated. By now all of these were also being offered in a walnut finish but for some indefinable reason on this variety of guitar it seemed to work, unless I've just warmed to it over the years. As with the SG range, Norlin had the notion of producing a cheap to build version of this format intended as a budget or entry level instrument. So it was that they came up with the ES320 in 1971. This was a totally new model and was not intended to replace another. It continued with the familiar 335 outline with two f-holes but was fitted with the same Melody Maker pickups and chrome surrounds carried over from the SG100 and SG200, together with the Telecaster style chrome plate fixed to the right hand lower bout. They were available in three finishes, natural, cherry and walnut. Although not quite as desirable as their big sister 335s they in fact played well, though the overall appearance wasn't to everybody's taste and the old single coil pickups were weak by comparison. These were discontinued in 1974, though some sources state 1975. A second totally new ES model was launched in 1972 and this one was designated ES325. This was more like a 335 in many respects but with some major twists, intended to cut costs. The stock 335 had a solid block running right through the body, intended to eliminate feedback, but the new 325 was hollow except for a half-block which was installed merely below the bridge and continued down to the tailpiece. It featured twin Firebird pickups with chrome covers and, as with those earlier SGs, had all the controls and jack socket pre mounted to a D shaped escutcheon plate. As this left no space for the f-hole on the right hand side of the body there wasn't one. Initially these were available in walnut or cherry, and a wine red option was offered as the decade progressed. Although they weren't perfect the 325s were pretty good guitars, sold quite well, and in fact were not discontinued until 1979, easily outlasting Norlin's other bargain basement efforts.

Kelly Rhodes and Pat Foley
with the original and prototype

Thanks to Pat Foley - Pat was Gibson's Artist Relations Manager and organised the Randy Rhodes re-issue. Pat quotes "This 1974 model was one of the success stories from the Norlin era, Kelly was a joy to work with on the project. Zakk Wylde who put me in touch with Randy's family and vouched for my credibility. He was very close with the family.
photo by the late Edwin Wilson

Things weren't all doom and gloom, however. Their cornerstone Les Paul series continued, the new Deluxe having been in production for a few years by this time, as had the Custom, by now available in a range of finishes rather than the traditional black. One noteworthy tweak on the Les Paul models of the time was the so-called sandwich, sometimes pancake, body. This was another way of reducing costs. The bodies were made from two pieces of mahogany with a narrow layer of maple between them using a process called cross-banding, the maple cap then adhered to the whole. Although there may well be the odd exception, guitar makers being the way they are, it now seems that all Les Paul's made between 1969 and 1976 used this process. The Pro Deluxe with two P90s appeared mid decade, as did a reissue Standard with two full humbuckers. There were also the three pickup Artisan and a handcrafted top of the range "The Les Paul" model amongst others.

The Norlin takeover gave Les Paul the opportunity to revitalize his relationship with Gibson. This had been strained throughout the sixties, and the decade didn't get off to a good start, as when he'd first caught sight of the new SG styled Les Paul range in 1961, he is widely reported as saying "What the f**k is that". The result was that he eventually had his name removed from them, and for most of the remainder of the sixties no guitars bearing his name were produced at all. Not a good outcome for a name that was once Gibson's big star and principal flag bearer. So along came Norlin who were seemingly not averse to introducing some new models and thus expanding the dated catalog that they'd inherited. They had much discussion with Les who was enthusiastic about making a guitar that would feature his much vaunted low impedance pickups. So, long story short, the Les Paul Personal and Les Paul Professional were released in 1969, and officially one year later in the UK and Europe. Initial reaction was, shall we say, muted. They had far too many knobs and switches, the walnut finish wasn't attractive, and the overwhelming majority of players who had no prior experience of low impedance pickups didn't fully understand what the purpose behind them actually was. They also required quite heavy transformer cables so the guitars could be used with conventional high impedance input amps. Added to that was the fact that these two guitars had bodies of Honduras mahogany that measured 14" across the lower bout, a full inch wider than many other Les Paul models. This made them heavy and rather cumbersome. The Personal featured gold plated hardware, and, oddly enough, a microphone input on the left side upper bout. All guitars were supplied new with a mike on a gooseneck type holder which would enable a soloist to move around the stage singing, but without having to be restricted by a static mike stand. The Professional had nickel plated hardware and thus was somewhat lower priced. All of these had onboard transformers so they could be switched from low to high impedance easily. Never particularly big sellers the Personal was discontinued in '73 after just 143 were made, and the Professional was too, but I have been reliably informed that production lumbered on until 1979, though by that time numbers had ebbed away to virtually zero. In total around 2300 Professionals were produced. Somewhat more palatable was the Les Paul Recording. Introduced in 1971. The body reverted to more acceptable dimensions, and the finish was a much paler shade of natural mahogany. It still had a confusing number of knobs and switches, so much so that Gibson was prompted into simplifying the control panel mid-decade. Other finishes became available as the decade advanced, white from 1975, cherry sunburst from 1976, ebony and dark walnut from 1978. Some globally famous players used the Recording, including Keith Richards, and most famously by Terry Kath of Chicago. It was a moderately good seller, though didn't set the world on fire. Sales allegedly peaked in '73, and by '78 it had been dropped from the roster, 5380 having been made. Although the guitar has been much maligned and criticized over the years, I think that over 5000 is an impressive number and it's worth bearing in mind that is three times as many as all of the '58, '59, and '60 series of Les Paul Standard "Bursts". Reissues of the Recording have been made subsequently so some people evidently love them. It all proved one thing, however, and it is that low impedance pickups do actually work, provided that you understand how they work and what they do. So, do these guitars represent an advance in the instrument's technology? Yes, I think they do, it's just that guitar players, being a conservative bunch, didn't take to them.

The RD series appeared, loosely based on the original Firebird body shape, and there were sporadic reissues of things like Flying V's and Explorers. Although the range of full bodied jazzers had been culled some were still being made, and we saw a thinline version of the ES175 designated ES175T, and even a solid bodied L5, designated L5S, very popular with a certain Ronnie Wood. There was also the L6S, similar silhouette but without the bling, and notable as being the first Gibson with a maple neck, and also the first with 24 frets. One new development was the Sonex, which had a wood core body coated in a plastic compound. It also featured something new to Gibson, a bolt on neck. To be fair it wasn't the prettiest guitar in the world, but I owned one for a couple of years, and feel-wise it was one of the best playing guitars I've ever had. The only problem was it looked as if it had been knocked together by my slightly nutty uncle in his garden shed. The fact remains though that some fine guitars were made during the period of Norlin oversight, and by the end of that decade there was a wider selection of models than there had been at the start, many of which have become desirable in the decades since and even reissued from time to time. Norlin were casting their net pretty wide in the '70s in a bid to produce saleable instruments, and to their credit came up with some innovative ideas. Sadly, though not all those ideas crossed over to become commercially successful. I'm not going to list all of those guitars here, there are far too many, and this is not a Gibson history book, so there won't be even the slightest reference to the Bicentennial Firebird of 1976 with its natural finish mahogany body and red, white, and blue Firebird logo.

Marauder

1974 Les Paul Standard
Raul Barrios

Gibson undeniably produced a lot of guitars during the years under Norlin's ownership, but there were times when they seemed to take their eyes off the ball. Well meant efforts at producing cheaper guitars, such as those we have reprised, had little impact and, as it turned out, proved to be expensive mistakes. None came close to projected sales targets, inventory piled up, and other models that appeared later in the '70s, such as the Sonex, Marauder, or S1 fared no better. Then came the '80s and the horror that was the Corvus (1982-1984) Why? That guitar, and others made alongside it, became the final nail in the coffin. By 1985 therefore, and owing to several other factors, Gibson and the Norlin parent were struggling and sailing close to bankruptcy, so in that year the Norlin era came to a close. Control and ownership passed on to a company headed by Henry Juszkiewicz, an enthusiastic guitarist with a career background centred in the auto industry, the brand began a rebirth and entered a new epoch. This began with the closure of the Kalamazoo factory and a move to Memphis and Nashville.

Les Paul Recording

1979 ES Artist
Ted Muir

80080130
Le Guitarium - Paris, France
Ben Brion photographer

1974 20th
Anniversary
John Cunningham

RD

1970
Gibson Crest
Dave Keeling

1974 ES-335 TD - # 397644
Kevin Roachford

1981 Heritage '10th built'

1975 Gibson Explorer in Mahogany - the serial is from 1975, which means it was a precursor to the 1976 Limited Edition Explorer made famous by The Edge of U2. Given that only 22 original Explorers were made in 1958 and 1959, it is probably one of the first 50 Explorers ever made by Gibson.

1976 Gibson Firebird III Bicentennial Edition this is the reissue of the '60s Firebird II timed to coincide with the USA's bicentennial celebrations.

969 Gibson Flying V in Walnut - one of only 35 made

1983 Gibson Custom Shop Explorer in Korina - It appears that Gibson made around 100 Custom Shop and 100 Heritage Edition Explorers in Korina in 1983. Both seem equally rare.

1983 Gibson Moderne Heritage Edition in Korina - Given that the Moderne likely never made it to production in the '50s, the 1983 reissue was the first issue of the guitar made from a solid piece of Korina

1983 Gibson Flying V Heritage Edition Prototype in Korina - The serial of this guitar is A012. The low 'A' serials tended to be prototypes that shipped with a Gibson prototype stamp on the headstock.

DEAN GUITARS

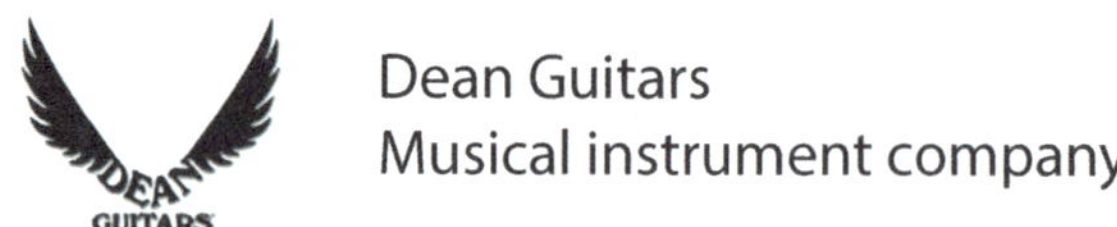

DEAN B. ZELINSKY

The Dean guitar brand was founded in Chicago in 1976 by Dean Zelinsky. It was pretty much a one man operation initially, and most of his early output was sold to musicians in the Chicago area, though his reputation for fine workmanship quickly became established, but even so relatively few Dean guitars were made during that early period. In 1986 the brand was sold to Oscar Medeiros (Note...sources vary on this date) who owned it until 1995 and then in 1997 Dean was sold to Armadillo Music which was owned by Elliott Rubinson, though Zelinsky himself was kept on a design consultant, and it was this particular change of ownership which launched the brand into the mainstream. It transpired that Rubinson happened to be the bass player with the Michael Schenker Group, and also with Uli Jon Roth, so it wasn't too long before Dean guitars found their way into the hands of these globally famous players. Other endorsees quickly followed, and it was a big list which included Leslie West and Dimebag Darrell. ZZ Top's famous rotating furry guitars were made by Dean. Aimed very much at the hard rock and headbangers market most Deans have extravagant body shapes based to some extent on Flying V's and Explorers, and all have an instantly recognisable large V shaped headstock, the outline echoed by the outspread angel-wing Dean logo. It must also be pointed out that Dean produces other more conservative designs as well, even including some acoustic models. Justifiably it can be said that the brand has developed into being one of the market leaders in that genre. All of their top-end electrics are currently being made at their Custom Shop facility in Tampa Florida, and a majority of their production models are now made in the Far East, principally Indonesia. Luna guitars are also owned by Dean. They produce an interesting range of decorative acoustic guitars, plus banjos. mandolins, and ukuleles. In 2008 Dean Zelinsky, being increasingly unhappy with the corporate business ethos, departed to form DBZ Guitars, Then, in 2012, he formed Dean Zelinsky Private Label. Once again he had a company over which he had total control.

Dean Prototype ML Carved Quilt Top
thanks to Taaha's Gear Locker -

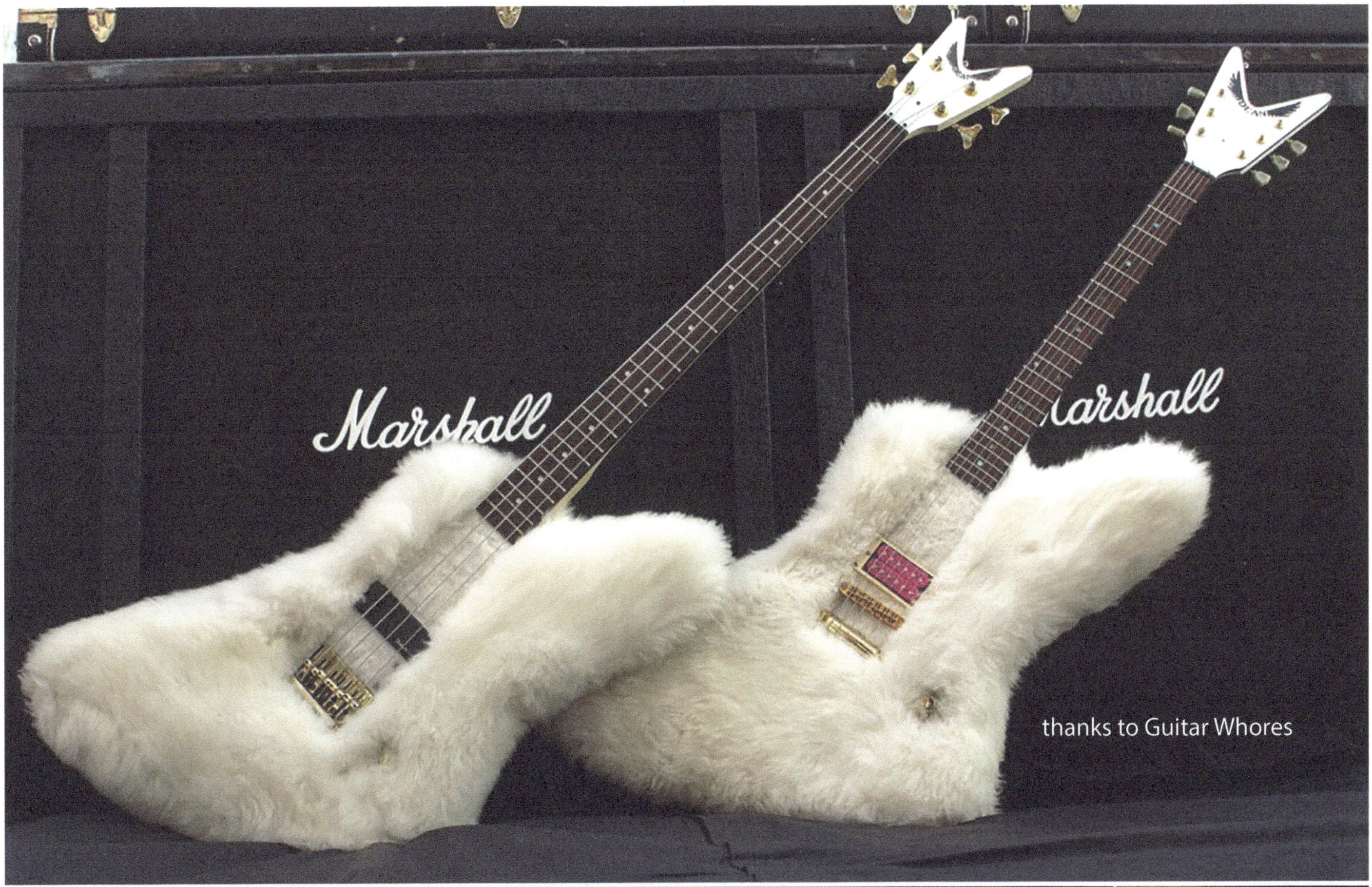
Marshall
arshall
thanks to Guitar Whores

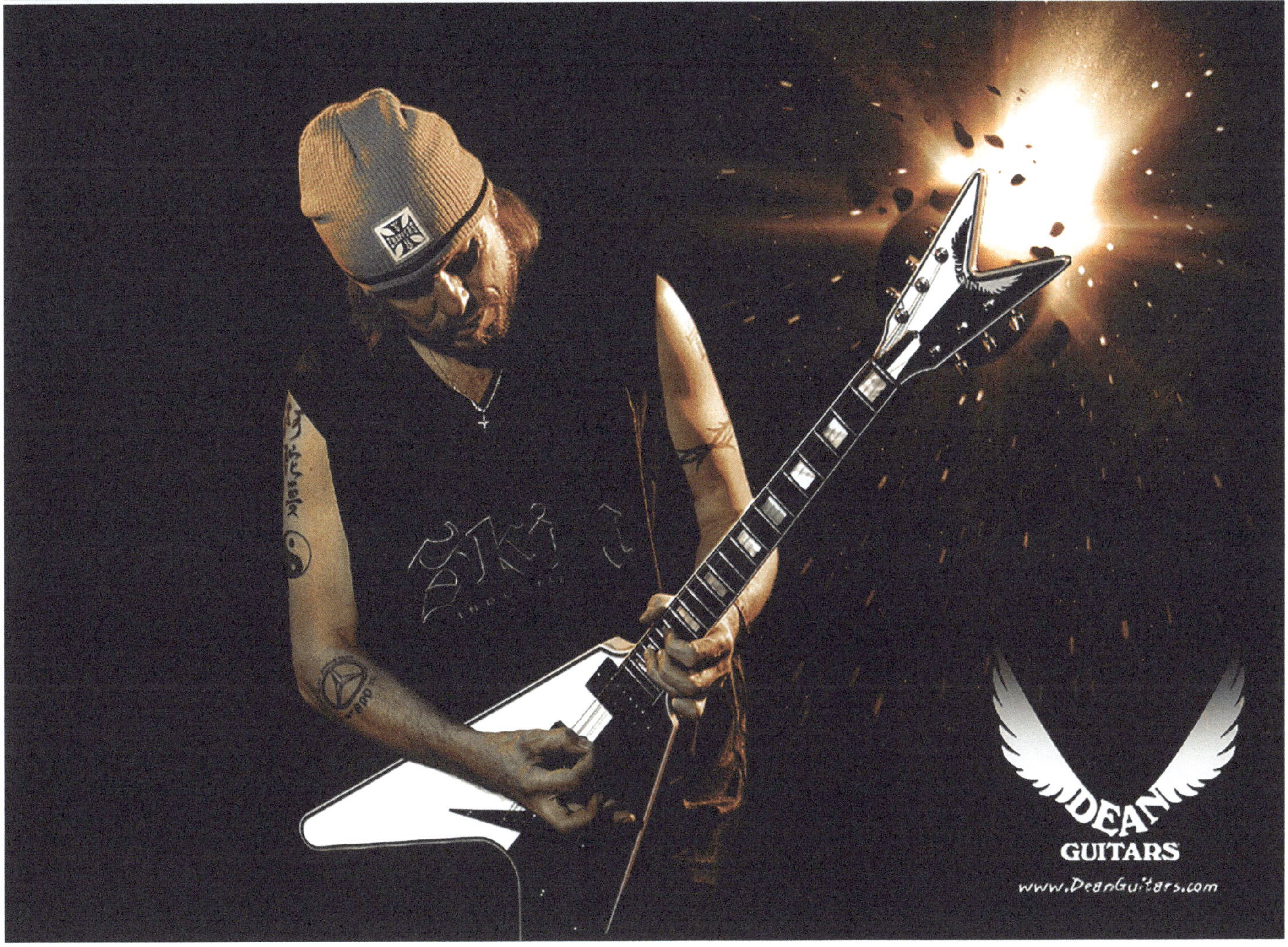
DEAN
GUITARS
www.DeanGuitars.com

STROMBERG

Elmer Stromberg son of Charles

Freddie Green and his Master 400

And what of Stromberg I hear you ask? As it was they who started this whole thing off there is no question that they deserve more space. So here's the backstory. That story begins in 1906 when Swedish immigrant Charles Stromberg came to the US and settled in Boston. With his two sons he founded a musical instrument company known as Charles Stromberg & Son. The sons were Harry and Elmer. To begin with, the company was making mandolins, banjos, and some drums, but as the guitar became more popular during the first quarter of the 20th century they produced these in increasing numbers. As stated earlier experiments in electric guitars eventually led to the 1928 Electro model. This wasn't a great success from a practical viewpoint however and no further experiments were made. The ever increasing demand for arch top jazz guitars for big bands however steered them in that direction, and they did have a head start, their first f-hole model being introduced in 1927, just four years after Lloyd Loar's first such, his Gibson L5. Elmer in particular turned out to be a superb craftsman and the guitars he personally made are reputed to be the best arch tops ever produced by anybody. Various models came and went, including the G1, G5 plus others in that series, and his Master 300 and Master 400 models. These were massive, with a 19 inch lower bout, and the volume they produced was much appreciated by guitarists of the day, many of whom had still not cottoned on to electrics. One was put to very good use by Count Basie guitarist Freddie Green, and it was he, more than anyone else, who increased the visibility of the Stromberg brand. Record keeping at the factory swung between very poor and nonexistent, thus nobody can be exactly sure how many Strombergs were made. My research during the compiling of this book has revealed figures from various sources varying between 340 and 640. I think the latter is more likely. Charles Stromberg died in 1955 and the company passed to Elmer. Tragically and unexpectedly he died later that same year, and that was the end of Stromberg. We have to fast forward at least a couple of decades when we discover that the Stromberg name, and all relevant legal rights, had been purchased by a company called NBE Corps based in Prague. A well known and long established manufacturer of guitars they own a large plant in Horovice in the Czech Republic. Stromberg brand instruments are now being produced again, in Europe now, and to very high standards. A part of the factory floor is shared with Maybach guitars. NBE are also making guitars for Jolano, a well known domestic brand, plus guitars sold under brands such as Esh, Clover, Spector, the current Brian May Specials are also made there, and, surprisingly certain Peavey models. The same factory is also home to NS Design, Ned Steinberger's current venture. Since 1990 Steinberger has been producing a line of solid body electric violins, violas, cellos, upright basses, plus one bass guitar, at their Horovice plant. No guitars just yet though.

Montreux - thanks to www.artofthearchtop.com

Stromberg Model G-3 Arch Top Acoustic Guitar, c. 1935, made in Boston, Mass., # 461, sunburst lacquer finish, maple back and sides, spruce top; laminated maple neck with ebony fingerboard thanks to Retro Fret

MARTIN ELECTRIC GUITARS

Martin guitars are best known for their extensive range of superbly built and legendary acoustic guitars. As the electric age really built up a head of steam, they felt they were missing out and saw a bandwagon that they could jump on to. The company had been manufacturing guitars since 1833 and are the oldest established brand name still active today, very close now to 200 years of continuous operation. And therein, lay the problem. For a company so identified with acoustic guitars to suddenly come out with electrics was an earthshaking change of direction. Would people accept them and warm to them? As it turned out the answer was no, despite several attempts and the launching of a range of models. The issue was one of marketing, and if they'd come up with a good snappy brand name for their electrics from the outset things might have turned out differently, but, as I've said before, hindsight is a wonderful thing. So, starting in the late '60s the first electrics were made. 1967 witnessed the arrivals of the GT-70 and GT-75 models. These were semi acoustic thin line guitars and looked a little Gretsch-y, although nowhere near what could be called copies. They were equipped with the redoubtable DeArmond pickups. I've actually played a couple of these, and they are in fact very nice guitars. Around 700 were allegedly made of each model. It was a slow start, and things didn't really get much better. Their next foray was in 1979 with the EM-18 solid body guitar and a companion EB-18 bass. The guitar had two humbuckers, and the bass one. A twin pickup EB 28 bass followed in 1983. They were nicely made, played well, and looked OK, though nothing new or out of the ordinary. In 2002 they released the AL-X7. This was a bit of an oddball. It was a slim body round hole semi acoustic with a single coil pickup close to the bridge. Didn't catch on. In 2004, they made their last electric, so far at least, an archtop jazz guitar named the CF-1. Very much a traditional arch top with f-holes, and a floating pickup, not at all unlike Gibson's Johnny Smith. Perhaps they'd have better luck aiming guitars at the lower end of the market, they reasoned, which is exactly what most of the other big names had done. Thus it was in 1985 they went to South Korea to have a range of cheap guitars made. These were sold under the brand name Stinger, and essentially, they were copied Fender Stratocasters with a restyled headstock and different finishes. This experiment lasted until 1996 at which point the range was discontinued.

1963 F 65 #193126 thinline
Two De Armond Dynasonic pickups
A total of 566 F 65s were shipped,
this is the only known 1963 lefty.
John Shannon

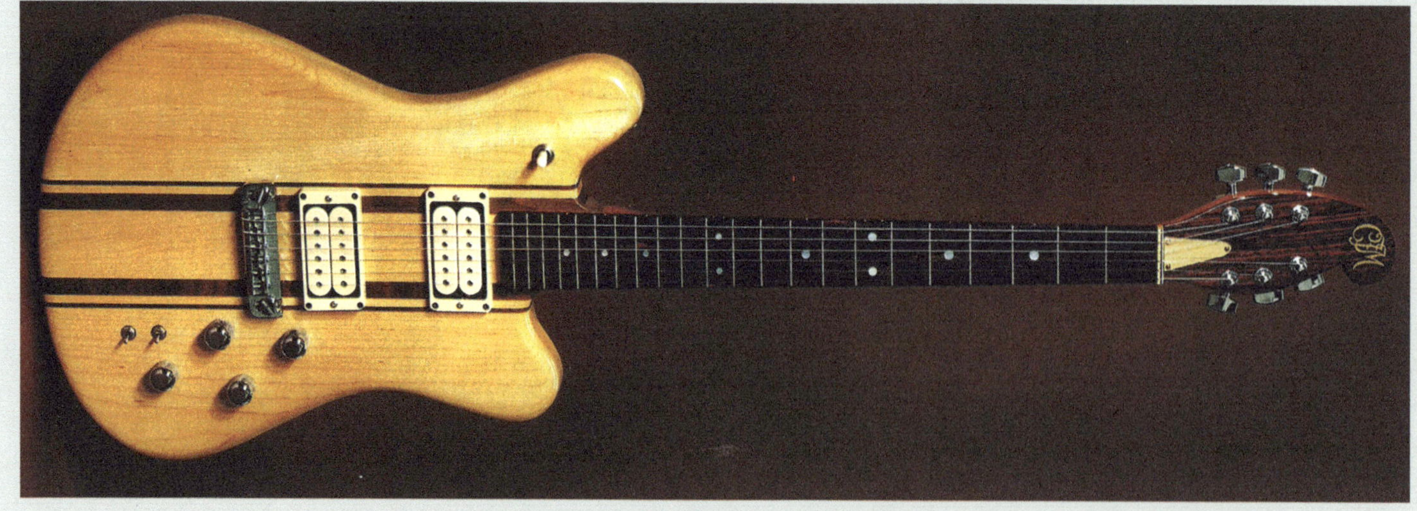

1960's MARTIN GT-75
w/DeArmond pickup

thanks to Olivia's Vintage

1979 MARTIN EM-18-natural Rumble Seat Music

BC RICH GUITARS

If you ever nurse a desire for a guitar with a quirky body shape, then you need to look no further than B C Rich. This brand was the brainchild of Bernard Chavez Rico, hence the B C Rich acronym. He spent his formative years in the '50s working in his father's East Los Angeles guitar shop. The shop primarily sold traditional classical Spanish and flamenco guitars, and Bernard became an accomplished flamenco guitarist. He became interested in electrics, and the way they were constructed, and in 1968 he made his first solid body guitar which followed, as usual, popular Fender outlines. By 1972 he was getting into his stride and came up with a guitar which he christened the B C Rich Seagull. The body style was unique and incorporated several pointy bits, which some players complained of as being uncomfortable. It was constructed following the thru-neck method, and worked well, aside possibly from the pointy bits, and by 1974 the Seagull was in full production which continued until the model was discontinued in '76. This was followed by the Eagle, basically an upgraded Seagull. The Eagle unusually for the time had 24 frets and onboard active electronics. There was also an Eagle Supreme which featured cloud fretboard inlays and body binding. Next came the Stealth which was designed by noted B C Rich devotee Rick Derringer. In 1976 the Mockingbird was added to the range, appearing initially as a short scale bass, the six string popping up a little later. Virtually all of B C Rich guitars made during this time were fitted with DiMarzio pickups and were hard-tail with a Leo Quan Badass bridge/tailpiece. After 1986 Rich started manufacturing their own pickups. In 1977 the extraordinary and unique Rich Bich appeared. This was a ten string guitar and strung just like a conventional 12 string but missing the octave A and bottom octave E string, in other words the 9th and 11th strings. The guitar featured a regular six string headstock with the additional four tuners fitted to the body just below the bridge. It wasn't uncommon to see players use these strung as a regular six string guitar. There were also a number of twin necks made, very heavy they are too. It is also worth pointing out that although all of the guitars mentioned were made in what essentially was a B C Rich Custom Shop, he was also having lower end models imported from South Korea. The story of Bernard and his company is turbulent and convoluted, even by the standards of the industry, and I'm not going down that road. Suffice to say that the brand had several different owners, and Bernard lost control of his own company more than once, though he always seemed to bounce back. Sadly, he passed away in 1999, but his name lives on with a range of instruments made in Asia. As far as his US originals are concerned, you either like them or you don't, but they certainly stand out from the crowd. It illustrates perfectly that one can make solid body electric guitars in any peculiar shape one wants to, provided you can physically pick them up and hold them, but they are always still guitars.

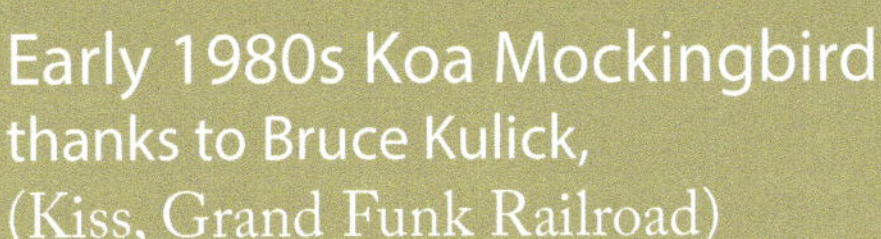

Early 1980s Koa Mockingbird
thanks to Bruce Kulick,
(Kiss, Grand Funk Railroad)

PRS PAUL REED SMITH GUITARS®

Paul Reed Smith, a keen guitarist, and another one of those guys who, from very humble beginnings came to be a leading name in the industry. As far back as the mid '70s he was tinkering with guitars and making his own while still at college. He graduated to his own properly equipped workshop in Annapolis Maryland, and by 1985 was ready to launch his first PRS brand guitar, which he did at the NAMM show of that year. Just three years later he was employing 45 staff and producing 15 guitars a day. By this time, he had met up with ex Gibson president Ted McCarty and McCarty had become his mentor, and frankly, PRS couldn't have found anyone better. In 1996 a bigger factory was located and production continued and increased. The PRS range consisted primarily of guitars loosely based on older Gibson outlines, not surprisingly, really taking into account McCarty's influence. The PRS double cut model was broadly similar to Gibson's 1959-60 style of Les Paul Special but now with a carved top, and the single cut had obvious echoes of a Les Paul Standard. Those echoes were strong enough to prompt Gibson to take legal action against PRS for copyright infringement. The resultant legal battle dragged on for six years, but it was a case that PRS ultimately won, though at times it looked like a close run thing. Paul Reed Smith's guitars drew attention from some legendary players, some of whom had artist endorsed models made in their honour, such as John Mayer, Carlos Santana, and my dear friend Bernie Marsden who recently passed away. All PRS pickups were wound in their own factory, aside from a small number of instruments fitted with Lindy Fralin units. The range of guitars included McCarty series models from 1994, both solids and semi-solids, and right up to the truly stunning, and expensive, Private Stock series. Paul RS certainly knew about wood, and how to use it in the best possible way as can be seen on those beautiful and desirable instruments. His desire to capture a slice of the lower end of the market resulted in the 2000 introduction of the Korean made CE series, at a much more affordable, and entry level prices. In 2009 a series of PRS amplifiers were added to the catalogue, and the name continues, ever onwards and upwards.

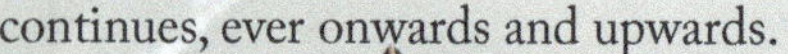

Bernie and Paul were close friends - Bernie endorsed PRS with his signature model.

John Mayer made the move to PRS and continues to endorse them. Above is the 'Dead Spec' model fitted with an Alembic Blaster pre amp. The guitar was used on the 2023 tour.
For the main photo we thank James Liverani

KRAMER GUITARS

As I wrote a few lines ago Gary Kramer, under somewhat acrimonious circumstances parted company with Travis Bean in 1976 and set up his own company. A close associate of his was Phillip J Petillo, who had been responsible for Travis Bean's prototypes and was now to work on Kramer's. Early run Kramer's borrowed a few tricks from Travis Bean, one of which was an aluminum neck, but this was a separate piece, unlike Bean's through-neck design. Kramer's was different in another respect in that the metal element of the neck was cast in a T cross section with a distinctive two prong headstock, and wood fillers were installed on each side of the neck. Kramer hoped that this would reduce weight, and would in part solve the very uncomfortable neck freeze issue if one was doing winter gigs in Minnesota.

This basic structural theme persisted across the Kramer range from 1976 until 1981, regardless of body style. In '81 Kramer began using a more conventional Stratocaster style wood neck, though this in turn led to a threat of litigation from Fender on the grounds of copyright infringement, so finally Kramer elected to go for the droopy banana style head which can still be seen to this day. Something extraordinary happened in 1978, and it was the release of the first Van Halen album. Once we'd all gone "Whaaaat" and picked ourselves up off the floor we all realised that a new approach to the guitar had emerged, and it was called shredding. Now it so happened that EVH's famous Frankenstrat guitar was a heavily modified Kramer, and the company soon capitalized on this and introduced a whole new line of guitars based on that very theme. Little was needed to make a guitar for shredders, and to say that they were minimalist is probably an understatement. All you needed was a Stratocaster style body, though other styles became available, a neck with a higher fret profile, just a single pickup close to the bridge, the most powerful one you can find, and what quickly became known as a Dive Bomber vibrato, an essential accessory which would enable said shredder to lower the pitch of the strings by a whole octave, or even more if required. Such units were being made in quantity by the early '80s by companies such as Floyd Rose and Kahler. Thus it was that Kramer started producing these guitars in quantity, mostly from imported Japanese parts that were simply assembled in the New Jersey factory. Unfortunately for Kramer such things don't last forever. The shredding fad diminished somewhat and their sales were flagging. Possibly a case of putting all one's eggs into one basket, the result being that Kramer was purchased by Gibson in 1991. Production of Kramer brand guitars continues, with models priced from beginners level up to mid range. I've just been through the price list and at the time of writing, prices run from around 200USD up to about 1000USD. Most of the current range are made in Gibson's Chinese Epiphone factory, though at times others have been made in Japan or Korea. The lower priced Kramer Pacer model is made in the Czech Republic. There have been many models in the Kramer range since 1976, by my count there are 74 including model variations, and obviously too many to list here.

1986 Eddie Van Halen autographed 5150 Tour Guitar
thanks to Kevin King Duggan

DMZ 3000 1970s
Gary Kramer built after he split with Travis Bean. It was the next progression of aluminum necked guitars.

NOTABLE DESIGNERS AND CHANGING CUSTOMER DEMANDS

During the sixty years or more that I have been involved with guitars, either as a player, a retailer, or a commentator, much has changed, conversely, there are things that haven't. There are many futuristic and extrovertly designed guitars available to those who aspire to such things, but, paradoxically many of those old cello style archtops also remain popular. It is plain to all of us that the market, over those decades, has been dominated by 'The Big Six' by which I mean Gibson, Gretsch, Epiphone, Rickenbacker, Fender, and Guild, the first four of whom were well entrenched prior to the Second World War. The modern guitar landscape, and I refer to the 1960s and later, features several brands who, although not around in the beginning, or one of the Big Six, nonetheless have their importance and deserve a place in this story. They also, both individually and collectively, sell a lot of guitars, and most of you readers will have owned one of these at some point. At its most basic level, a guitar is what it is. It has six strings. a neck and fretboard, and an ergonomically shaped body that sits comfortably on your thigh. Tastes change, however, and fads come and go. Music changes too, and the dynamic of that can drive performance, thus it is that some guitarists might desire an instrument that is, shall we say, a bit more flashy. As a consequence, we have seen over the years some pretty weird guitars, the novelty of which usually fades quickly. From the standpoint of musical evolution, two decades elapsed between Scotty Moore and Angus Young, and two decades between T Bone Walker and Jimi Hendrix. That's not very long, and things can move remarkably quickly. Those great musicians inevitably required different results from their instruments. and all manufacturers have fought to keep abreast of those requirements. So here's my review of lesser known names, some that glowed only briefly, some never took off at all, and some that have managed to become established and respected over the years. They all have one thing in common, they had a great idea which seemed right at the time.

JAMES TYLER GUITARS

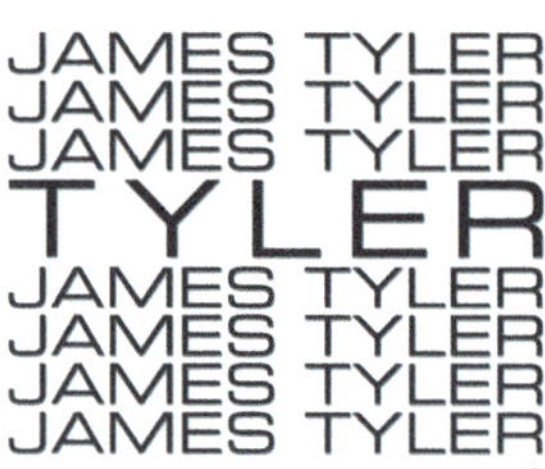

One of those guys, and tinkerers, as a high school kid in LA, James Tyler was constantly taking guitars to bits and putting them back together. He built up a solid reputation as a repairer and ended up working at the renowned vintage guitar retailer Normans Rare Guitars as a repairer and restorer. He finally got his own workshop in 1980 and started work building his own branded guitars, the first of which debuted in 1987. His company has gone from strength to strength, and he claims that although he uses the most technologically up to date production machinery his guitars are all finished and set up by hand to ensure the very best quality. He now has a larger factory and also has a cheaper line of guitars made by Kitahara Gakki in Japan. His guitars recall familiar Fender outlines, but with some artistic and unique finishes.

A Dan Huff model that was built for a NAMM show in the mid '90s and imported to the UK.
thanks to Derek Mcnair

CHARVEL GUITARS

Both Charvel and Jackson have become prominent names in the guitar fraternity, and, as their stories are so closely intertwined, the only logical way to view those stories is to combine them.

Wayne Charvel worked for the Fender company between 1971 and 1973 but opened up his own workshop in 1974. Initially, he was doing repairs and modifications but he soon branched out into making his own complete Charvel branded guitars, often from proprietary parts. Unfortunately, in 1978 he'd become bankrupt and sold his business to one Grover Jackson, and that included the rights to the Charvel brand name. Jackson had his own ideas and was targeting his guitars very much at the heavy rock and metal market well on the ascendant by this time. Indeed one of his very first production guitars was the arrow shaped Randy Rhoades, made in response to an approach from Randy himself. This was also known as the Concorde model. A whole range of other models followed over the years, far too many to list individually here. but it was very obvious what his target market was, droopy headstocks and all. In 1986 production of Charvel brand guitars ceased, though the Jackson brand continued for a while longer, by this time including the budget priced bolt on neck Dinky series.

In 1989 Jackson sold Charvel/Jackson to a Japanese company, and from then until 1991 all guitars were made there. Charvel/Jackson was purchased by Fender in 2002, and since then a range of limited editions have been released. Both Wayne Charvel and Grover Jackson had identified their potential consumers correctly and sold a lot of guitars. Indeed they still do, so they deserve full marks for that. Limited space precludes me from listing and picturing all of their models manufactured over so many years, there are literally far too many, and this isn't a guitar catalog.

1990 Charvel Surfcaster 12 String thanks to Vintage and Modern Guitars

HAMMER GUITARS

As I write this book it is a constant surprise to me just how many of our best known and sought after guitar brands are begun by a guy, or a couple of guys, tinkering about with guitars in their own homes, schools, or small workshops. who then turn out to have exceptional talent and skill, and see their try-outs and tinkerings blossom into full blown guitar factories employing large numbers of people who produce hundreds, or even thousands, of instruments a year. In that sense, Hamer is no exception. The Hamer name has a fifty plus year history, with several changes of factory location, and key company employees who came and went during that period. My space here is limited, so for the sake of brevity, I will condense the fifty years down somewhat. The two key players in the saga are Jol Dantzig and Paul Hamer. In 1973 they opened a music store in Wilmette Illinois called Northern Plains Music. The collector's vintage guitar trade hadn't really gained full momentum at the time, but it seems that Dantzig foresaw what was coming and squirreled away rare Fender Broadcasters, Les Paul Standards and suchlike as and when they cropped up in the shop. At some point it occurred to them that they could make guitars just as good, "new vintage" guitars in effect, but at a fraction of the price of the originals. Choosing Hamer as a brand name simply because it sounded better they made their first guitar in 1973, which was a short scale Flying V bass. Their second followed a year later and was a reproduction of the Gibson Explorer, but had improved on the original by having a flame maple top cap and bound edge body. Jol used the bass himself on stage and it wasn't long before people were asking what the guitar was, thus the name started to spread around the musical community, and by 1975 Hamer were receiving their first orders. Travelling all around the country, attending gigs, and even placing Hamer guitars in the hands of famed players, such as Rick Nielsen, Mick Ralphs and Rick Derringer amongst many other worthies. Hamer guitars were targeted very much at the heavy rock and headbangers market, being primarily Explorer shaped or V shaped, but as time passed the fad was wearing off a little and by '77 Hamer found themselves struggling, causing Dantzig to have to start selling off his vintage guitar collection just to stay afloat. They introduced what turned out to be their very successful Sunburst model. This was based on the outline of the '59 and '60 Gibson Les Paul Junior and Special body style but with a carved maple cap like a Les Paul Standard.

More new guitars appeared in the '82 model year and Hamer had seemingly turned a corner. A line of budget priced Hamer's were contracted out to a Korean manufacturer in the '90s, and that continued until 2002 at which point production was sourced from China or Indonesia until 2012. Good things don't last forever though, and in 1988 Hamer was sold to the Kaman Corporation, owners of Ovation, and Hamer production moved to Kaman's east coast plant. Kaman, in turn, was acquired by Fender in 2007 and in 2012 it was announced that all Hamer production would cease. In 2017 we began to see Asian made imports, probably Chinese, of Hamer guitars made to original designs, so the name lives on.

Cheap Trick on stage in 1977 with their Hamer instruments: Rick Nielsen (left) with a standard model and Tom Petersson with a 10-string bass
Carl Lender

Paul Stanley, Kiss and a collection of guitars from Seymour Duncan

PARKER GUITARS

Our story has propelled us into the 1990s, and you could be forgiven for assuming that all the development, innovation, and evolution of the guitar had already reached its zenith, and there was nowhere left to go. Then the Parker Fly appeared.

Ken Parker, a native of Long Island, in association with Larry Fishman, he of acoustic guitar transducer fame, had formed a company to make guitars. Parker was a guitar repairer, inventor, and keen guitarist, who thought he could make better guitars than the big boys. He had several unique, new ideas, and in 1991 started work on prototypes. Some of his ideas were indeed totally new, and the processes necessary to begin production, the special tooling needed for example, and the research and development required, took a little while, and in fact his first Fly guitars didn't become available until 1993. The final product was named The Fly due to its bold and instantly recognisable body and headstock style. Necks and bodies were of woods such as mahogany, poplar, basswood, and rosewood, and the choice of tonewood depended upon the specific model. Bodies also featured a carbon fiber composite exoskeleton. This gave the bodies more strength and rigidity, therefore enabling the body mass to be reduced resulting in an extremely lightweight instrument. A Fly body weighed around four and a half pounds or two kilos, easily half the weight of most other popular guitars at the time. Fretboards were epoxy with a graphite nut, and, on most models, were equipped with 24 stainless steel frets. The frets had no tangs and were applied flat side to the fretboard using a special adhesive. The vibrato unit was made in such a way that allowed it to move up and down as most such units do, or be set to a dive only setting to keep the Van Halen fans happy, or it could be locked in position serving as a static bridge. All Parker Fly's were fitted with Fishman transducers which required an on board preamp powered by a nine volt battery. Thus a Fly could be played as a conventional electric, or as a convincing acoustic, or the two sources mixed allowing the player an unrivalled tonal soundscape. All pretty clever stuff and the final production guitars incorporated no less than eleven of Parker's own patents. Pickup offerings varied. The Fly Deluxe for example had a poplar body, basswood neck and DiMarzio pickups, whilst the Fly Mojo had a mahogany neck and body with Seymour Duncan pickups. The Fly range consisted of ten models. Two were mentioned earlier, and added to those were the Classic, Midi (with two single coils and a bridge humbucker), Artist, Supreme, Nite, Concert, later renamed Bronze, a nylon strung Spanish model, and a bass which had a slightly wider and fatter body. A Mojo Midi was also produced in the early '90s which sported two DiMarzio humbuckers. As the name suggests the midi equipped guitars could be interfaced with a synthesizer or some other form of midi controller. All of that technology was still very new and revolutionary back in the '90s, though fairly commonplace now. Ken Parker seemed always to be ahead of the curve. The Fly was well received generally, and many of the decades top names bought and used them regularly. One outstanding player was ex Frank Zappa and King Crimson guitarist Adrian Belew, and for a while Parker produced a version of their Deluxe model as an Adrian Belew Edition, so that would make eleven models in total.

In spite of all of that inventiveness and genius on the part of Ken Parker and Larry Fishman, there were dark clouds gathering on the horizon. One factor appears to be a few intrinsic design flaws. The graphite nuts wore down quite quickly and were also prone to coming loose. The rather clever vibrato unit contained ball bearings which were likely to drop out, and did. Most threatening of all though was the pricing structure. Despite selling 30,000 guitars during their existence the company was never profitable. It has been said that Parker were making $10,000 guitars which, because of the way the market was, had to be sold for $2000. This situation became untenable and in 2003 Parker sold his company to MusicCorp. Shortly thereafter, and not wishing to become part of the corporate treadmill Ken Parker departed. In 2009 the brand was sold once more to Jam Industries, and by 2016 it was reported that the brand was moribund. Ken moved to Massachusetts where he now makes fine quality archtop jazz guitars that still feature that iconic and recognizable Fly headstock. The Fly guitar was indisputably memorable and contained several unique features. You could, with some justification, say that it was a product of vision but ultimately failed due to economic pressures and market dynamics. A flash in the pan? Yes, maybe, but I think they are better than just that. It's a tough world out there.

This is the original early version that Ken Parker built when he launched the company. The redwood necks and poplar bodies create a very lively instrument, but there was a problem with mass producing them that way, some redwood necks created ghost notes, and the employees of the newly formed Parker company spent a day in the parking lot, smashing the bad ones, while it is estimated that 60 or so of the good ones survived.
This guitar was born on July 19, 1993, and it was the 2nd guitar built that day.

Jacques Menache

thanks to Jacques Menach

VELENO

John Veleno, of St Petersburg Florida was an engineer and machinist working for NASA. He was also a guitarist, and it occurred to him that it would make a lot of sense to make a guitar from aluminum. He wasn't the first person to make such a guitar, nor would he be the last. Working mainly from home he did everything himself and had no employees. His first prototype was finished in 1967. It was a symmetrical double cutaway body with a flat top, two humbuckers, and a bolt on neck, also milled from solid aluminum, thus it needed no truss rod. The headstock swept up into a sharp twin pointed V, ideal for dissuading an over enthusiastic fan who might jump on to the stage. The first Veleno production models were offered in 1971, and around 200 were eventually made. Their very unique tone caught on, and some very major names owned one. There were variations, a couple had three pickups, subtle variations in body outline crept in, and some had a colored anodised finish. There were some undocumented one offs as well, so 200+ would be more accurate. The Veleno company has recently been revived, and their website is currently taking orders. I've been lucky enough to have encountered two of these, and they were indeed something very special. Veleno undeniably deserves his piece in this jigsaw puzzle.

1971 Veleno Traveller ex Peter Haycock - ATB Guitars

MESSENGER GUITARS

Next is the short lived Messenger, and if it wasn't for its use by Mark Farner of Grand Funk Railroad the brand might have passed unnoticed. it was a slim semi acoustic, with barely any cutaways, and featured an aluminum neck. It also had a built in fuzztone, unusual though not unique. These guitars were made in Astoria Oregon merely from 1967 to 1968. Currently the Eastwood company is offering a reproduction of this guitar.

THE ELECTRICAL GUITAR COMPANY (EGC)

This company was founded in the mid 1980s by a player named Kevin Burkett, who really loved his Travis Bean, and the unique tone and sustain it gave him. He got some money together and started building his own aluminum (in the US aluminum) guitars. Now I usually avoid letting my personal opinions color in any way what I write, but these guitars are simply drop-dead gorgeous. If I wasn't retired now, I'd buy one in a heartbeat. He is currently based in Alabama, having moved from Pensacola Florida, and produces instruments in several body styles, which include a Telecaster. a Jazzmaster, a Mosrite, and of course the Travis Bean amongst others. He also makes guitars with acrylic bodies. All are available in six string, baritone, or bass types. Spare bolt on necks too if you want them. 1600 instruments out of the door so far, and long may that continue.

SD CURLEE GUITARS

The S D Curlee guitar company was the brainchild of three friends from Matteson IL, Randy Curlee, a bass player, Randy Dritz, an instrument designer, and Sonny Storbeck, a woodworker and pattern maker. They thought it would be a sensible and logical plan to build basses and guitars, simply and cheaply, that most people could easily afford. Thus it was in 1976 that they built their first bass. It was made with a natural wood finish, very trendy at the time, and although it had a through neck appearance did in fact have a bolt on neck. Their instruments were well liked by local musicians so production moved into a higher gear fairly quickly and in the early days a considerable number of instruments were built at Matteson. Curlee had exactly the same problem that was affecting all other American makers at the time, which was the easy availability of cheap Japanese imports which undercut US retail prices by quite a margin. His solution was in fact a very clever one. He would import ready made necks and bodies from Japan, as it turned out these were to come from Hondo, then finish them in the Matteson workshop, just adding all the hardware, DiMarzio pickups, stringing them up, all then tuned and ready to go. Overall cost savings would be significant, and what, in a roundabout way, might be described as an American made guitar would be offered at a very affordable price. This plan proceeded well for a time, the basses becoming particularly sought after, and outselling six stringers by a ratio of five to one. However, as the years passed tastes changed, and that stripped back woody appearance became much less trendy and sales tanked. Curlee did make a last-ditch effort to produce some models with flashier and more colourful finishes, but it was too little too late, and the company folded in 1982. It is claimed, though it must be said disputed, that Curlee produced 15,000 instruments during its six and a half years existence. That equates to about 440 a week, in reality, quite a lot for a small operation. The basses went on to be very desirable, and eventually became collector's items, often changing hands for significant sums. The S D Curlee brand name was purchased in 2011 by Texas based entrepreneur and luthier Scott Beckwith of Birdsong Guitars, and limited production resumed after a long hiatus. During my research, I'd discovered that around 25 instruments are produced per year. Randy Curlee passed away in 2005. In mid 2024 I had a very cordial email from Scott informing me that no further examples would be made, and the S D Curlee brand was to be discontinued.

1976 SD Curlee Liberty-Bell-bass, natural
Southern Elk Music Co.

1977 SD Curlee Standard bass featuring a mahogany body, maple neck, and DiMarzio Brick pickup. Brass trimmings, because hey, it was the '70s - plus early poster
quote and thanks, Eric Ernest

G & L GUITARS

In 1980 Leo Fender and his long time associate George Fullerton decided to create a new guitar brand which they christened G&L Guitars, George and Leo. By this time Leo Fender had extricated himself from Musicman, and happily found himself the owner of the old Musicman factory in Fullerton. Guitar production was soon in progress, G&L body designs aping Leo's original Stratocaster, Telecaster, and Precision Bass. There were, however, or so it was claimed, a few fundamental improvements on Fender's original instruments. The first of these was the dual-fulcrum vibrato system. As we are all painfully aware when a vibrato arm is operated the strings almost never return to pitch. Leo figured that the more moving parts you had in any such unit the more likely this was to occur. He designed a unit, the main block of which rocked at just two points, the dual fulcrum in other words. This has actually been adopted now by many manufacturers, including on certain current Fender brand guitars. The next was the Saddle Lock bridge. As you all know Stratocaster and Telecaster pattern bridge saddles, whether on a Fender guitar or not, occasionally tend to move sideways. The Saddle Lock bridge had a small Allen screw on the sides so they could be locked in position. He also designed a practical kind of tilt neck mechanism to avoid the necessity of removing the neck and using shims if one ever needed to modify the neck pitch. Furthermore, there was his Bi-Cut neck. This was where the neck was assembled lengthwise in two halves with the truss rod enclosed within those halves. As the fretboard still had to be glued into place I, for one, can't quite understand what the purpose of this might have been. Upon the advent of modern CNC machines, the process became redundant anyway. Lastly was the Magnetic Field Design Pickup. Most modern guitar pickups use Alnico magnets. This is an acronym for ALuminiumNIckelCObalt, Alnico, get it? This alloy varied in proportion according to the individual manufacturer but was generally between around 30% and 60% of the total magnet weight, the remaining percentage being made up of iron. Leo knew how the magnets could have a bearing on the sound of a pickup, taking due account of other factors too, and made a decision to make his magnets from pure iron, and made in the way that pickups used to be made back in the '50s, and earlier. Leo called his G&L guitars the best guitars he'd ever made. Anyhow, leaving all of the technical stuff aside Leo sadly died in 1991, and his widow Phyllis took control of the company in partnership with George Fullerton. George died in 2009, and Phyllis in 2020. The G&L marque continues however, currently producing an American made Legacy series, and their budget Tribute range, initially made in South Korea from 2003, but now made in Indonesia. G&L guitars sell steadily and undoubtedly have a significant fan base, but will never put much of a dent in Fender sales, as illogical as that may seem. Incidentally, I've come across internet chatter from those who think that as George Fullerton lived and worked in a town named Fullerton, it is often assumed that the town was named in honour of him. I can assure you that it is a complete coincidence. George was born in Arkansas, and the town of Fullerton was founded in 1887 by a totally different Mr. Fullerton.

THE CHOICE OF
THE PROFESSIONAL
The G&L L2000 E BASS
MUSIC SALES, INC.
In to the future...
from out of the past.
MUSIC SALES, INC
LEGACY

schecter
guitar research

In 1976 David Schecter opened up a small repair shop in Van Nuys California. He had previously been living in Boston and at that time was working in an auto body shop. Whilst there he started building guitars for friends, using the auto shop's paint spraying facility to finish the bodies and necks. Once in Van Nuys he soon took on Tom Anderson in 1977, and it was he who mentored Schecter and taught him a great deal about guitars and how to build them. Anderson himself went on to be a highly respected boutique guitar maker. Schecter at this time concentrated primarily on building parts that he would sell to other makers, both ESP and Wayne Charvel could be counted among his customers. It wasn't until 1979 that his first Schecter brand guitars were made, leaving aside his earlier efforts from the Boston auto body shop period. His first instruments consisted of a Telecaster body style guitar, followed by a Stratocaster body style model, following the pattern of several other guitar builders at that time, and keeping to safe, conservative, and saleable, designs. Not everyone wants a guitar shaped like a squashed bug on a windshield. As with certain other makers described within these pages, his instruments were well made, well received, and by 1983 Schecter was struggling to cope with demand. It could justifiably be said that he was a victim of his own success, and in that same year, his company was bought out and moved to Dallas. From that point on David Schecter was to have nothing more to do with the guitars that still bore his name. Once in Dallas, the new Texan owners increased the range but still stuck firmly to the T style guitar which they christened the Saturn, and the S type, now named the Mercury. Fender took exception to this constant copying of their designs, and, as they had previously done with other makers, and were to do again in the future, commenced legal action against Schecter. This cost Schecter a lot of money and a cessation in production, and as a result the company folded in 1986. Just one year later the Schecter marque and all rights attached to it, were bought by a Japanese manufacturer named Shibuya. who already owned ESP. The primary production facility was moved back to California where the Schecter brand was mainly focused on building high-end guitars at their Custom Shop, producing around 40 guitars a month. To grab their fair share, of the budget end of the market production of their Diamond line began in South Korea in 1998. And so it continues. Over the years a great many Schecter models have come and gone, and I can't list them all here. I did try to count them all but I got to about 80 and gave up. One that stuck out for me though was the Schecter Hellraiser. What a perfect name for a guitar. We've come a long way indeed from Charlie Christian.

a NAMM special, thanks to Eric Ernest

Schecter Omen-7 Series Electric Guitar
thanks to Music Village

Schecter ST Vintage White late '80s, thanks to Guitarren Total

Wurlitzer is of course best known for jukeboxes, cigarette vending machines, and those massive white cinema and theatre organs, but they have also made guitars, although technically speaking they didn't actually make them themselves but had that done by somebody else who just stuck the Wurlitzer name on them. There are acoustic guitars bearing the Wurlitzer brand dating back to the early '20s that were made for them by C F Martin. It is however electrics that interest us here, and three Wurlitzer branded solid bodies appeared in 1965, the Wildcat, the Gemini, and the Cougar. These are quite handsome looking guitars actually, having a Harmony or Kay vibe about them, but that was the norm then, otherwise fairly run-of-the-mill. They were manufactured by a Kansas based company known as Holman Woodell. They were gone by 1968, so production of those guitars can't have lasted very long, three years at the most, so relatively few were ever made so don't feel bad if you've never seen one. I certainly haven't. Wurlitzer ended up in bankruptcy and was purchased by Gibson in 2001.

1960s Wurlitzer Wildcat
Monterey Park Guitar Shop

We are indebted to Adam who has done so much research of the Wurlitzer guitar - please visit the website for full information www.wurlitzerguitars.com

Gemini
Pulse Beat Guitars

The jukebox is an original 1945 Wurlitzer model 1015 "The Bubbler'. thanks to Jacques Menache
1966 Rickenbacker 365 in Fireglo.

Thin Cutaway 7741 Cherry 7742 Sunburst

1968-7741-Thinline-Redburst
Southside Guitars

BOND GUITARS

Bond

One day around 1975 or so I was quietly sitting in the shop, probably polishing something, when a gentleman came in with an acoustic guitar to which was attached a very odd fingerboard, and of a type I'd never seen before. It was made from aluminum and had no frets. Where the frets would have been were ridges, so if you viewed the fingerboard from the side, you would see an extended sawtooth pattern. He told me that it was a prototype and asked me what I thought. I played it for a couple of minutes and found it to be quite fast, especially playing a run going up the fingerboard. Not quite so easy when it came to bending notes, but I think some practice would be needed and a mere couple of minutes was not enough. However, I complimented him on his inventiveness and off he went. That gentleman was Bond, Andrew Bond. What I'd seen was indeed a prototype and in the fullness of time led to the eventual unveiling of the Bond guitar. In 1984 Bond had bought a small factory in a village about nine miles from Inverness in Scotland and had begun to make a guitar which he'd christened the Bond Electraglide. It had a double cutaway body with three single coil pickups, a vibrato, and a body and neck moulded from carbon fiber. It had on board active electronics, the power pack for which was contained in a separate box that sat beside you when on stage. And of course, there was the fretless ridged fingerboard that I'd seen about ten years previously. On paper this seemed to be a great idea, fundamentally changing the guitar and the way it was to develop in the future, at least it seemed so on paper. Although there were several big name players who warmed to the Bond, including The Edge from U2, they were in a very small minority and the overwhelming majority of players simply didn't take to it. It had a radically different feel which was well out of most guitarists' comfort zone. Even when I'd seen the prototype I'd instantly spotted one fatal flaw. Frets wear down and need to be replaced. Those ridges would have worn down too and developed depressions in exactly the same way frets do. When that happened, the only remedy would be to replace the entire fingerboard, not much use in twenty years' time when the company would likely have gone out of business. Bond ceased production in 1986 after a mere two years. To give Bond due credit, it's noteworthy ideas like his which, over many decades, have advanced the instrument to the point where we are now. Not all great ideas work out in practice, this being a prime example, and, unfortunately for Mr. Bond, his guitar just didn't take off, despite having a number of enthusiastic adherents. I have tried to garner information on production totals to no avail, but my best guesstimate would be somewhere in the low hundreds. Andrew Bond sadly died in 1999, and that, unfortunately, was the end of that. This original Bond company has no connection whatsoever with another company of the same name currently making guitars in Ukraine.

Bond Electraglide

thanks to Guitar Gavel

thanks to Paul Beardow

MATON GUITARS

Bill May

In compiling this volume I have forensically researched and examined every guitar brand that I can think of that has existed during the course of the last one hundred years. If I've overlooked one or two you have my humble apologies. The results of all of that I now pass on to you, the reader. As we all know the principal impetus and momentum of the electric guitar's development sprang from the USA. Aside from that though many interesting, innovative, and fine quality instruments have emerged from the UK, Japan, European countries such as Italy, Sweden, and Germany amongst others, and latterly many countries in the Indo-Pacific region. It would therefore be remiss of me not to turn my attention to Australia and the significant contribution that the nation has made to the overall picture. Leaving to one side the boutique and custom builders there are in Australia, and there are quite a few, one brand has emerged above all, has achieved a reputation that extends globally, and that brand is Maton.

In telling the over 80 year long history of Maton I have had the invaluable assistance of Maton employee Rob Marsh. I first met Rob over 50 years ago and it's sheer good luck that he now works for that company. As with any research of this kind access to the many sites on the internet is useful, and provides a good starting point. The information offered on those sites however is often contradictory or inaccurate, should never be entirely relied upon, and more in depth investigation is usually required to ensure accuracy, and that is why Rob's input has been so valuable with regard to Maton.

The Maton company has its origins in Melbourne and was solely due to the talents of Bill May. He was a luthier and a competent jazz guitarist who repaired guitars in his Melbourne workshop. He also custom built the occasional guitar, generally flat top round hole acoustics or nylon strung classical guitars, plus the occasional ukelele. He traded using his brand of Ma-Ton, also often written May-Tone. As we have seen so many times before in this industry his reputation for craftsmanship spread and in due course he was receiving increasing numbers of orders. He eventually enlisted the support of his brother Reg and by 1946 the Maton brand was in full production mode. In 1949 they incorporated the company name as the Maton Musical Instrument Company and moved to larger premises, still in the same area, and that new site was to serve him well for the next 40 years.

Bill had long been interested in electric guitars, still very new at that point, and had carried out various experiments throughout the '40s in an attempt to find something practical and saleable. His first successful electric guitar was made in 1954, and following the American pattern was an f-hole arch top with an added single coil pickup. This instrument however never went into full production. Oddly enough the manufacture of Maton amplifiers commenced in that same year, although a comprehensive range of electrics was still some years away. His early amps took on a similar aesthetic to certain contemporary American made amps, such as the Epiphone Electar, and Gibson models such as those old GA10's and GA20's. (continued on page 173)

The Hawaiian Swingtet onboard SS Chusan 1968, cruising from Sydney. Alan Whitely seen with the Maton he purchased in Melbourne. Author David Plues with Epiphone Riviera, Tom Plues with homemade Hawaiian which he would replace with a factory built model (also bought in Melbourne).

Maton Starline 4606

a stunning collection from a friend who wishes to remain anonymous

Maton

TICO MORELL, SYDNEY:
"A beautiful guitar in every sense."

DON ANDREWS AND BOB GIBSON ADMIRE THE "MATON MAYFAIR."

JOHN EDGECOMBE, SYDNEY GUITARIST:
"Maton guitars have everything a professional guitarist needs."

NEV. HARLAND, SYDNEY:
"The greatest rhythm guitar I have ever played."

ROY CAMPBELL, ADELAIDE COWBOY GUITARIST.

"My 'Mayfair' is the easiest guitar I have ever played."

Page Eight

Maton

ROY ROYSTON, SYDNEY GUITARIST AND TEACHER:
"I have tried them all and my 'Maton Sterling' more than compares with the best of them."

CLIFF ADAM, TEACHER AND PROFESSIONAL GUITARIST, WESTERN AUSTRALIA:
"I find Maton guitars have quality tone in all registers, and above all, rhythmic cutting power so essential."

BUDDY WILLIAMS, COWBOY STAR OF STAGE, RADIO AND RECORDS:
"My Maton, a great and magnificent guitar."

BUD BAKER, GRAHAM BELL'S WORLD-FAMOUS AUSTRALIAN JAZZ BAND:
"I have heard them all over the world, but my 'Mayfair' has a tone to beat them all."

Page Nine

BB 120

George Golla - I had the pleasure of seeing George and Don Burrows performing in the Wentworth Hotel Sydney in 1969, and still have the signed L.P. (DP)

George Harrison with the borrowed Maton

(continued from page 170)

They were covered in brown leatherette, the cabinets looking somewhat like home radios of the period. Their first amp kicked out a thumping four and a half watts. All of the electrical components were subcontracted out to the Philips Electrics Company, and the completed chassis were then installed into the cabinets which Maton made in house. As the rock and roll phenomenon arrived more volume was demanded, thus the range of Maton amps grew which included more conventional, even generic looking models, which of course became progressively louder, culminating in separate heads and cabinets. By the early '70s, and in common with so many other amplifier makers, Maton found themselves struggling in what was then a very competitive and crowded marketplace and amp production finally terminated in 1974.

EG-240

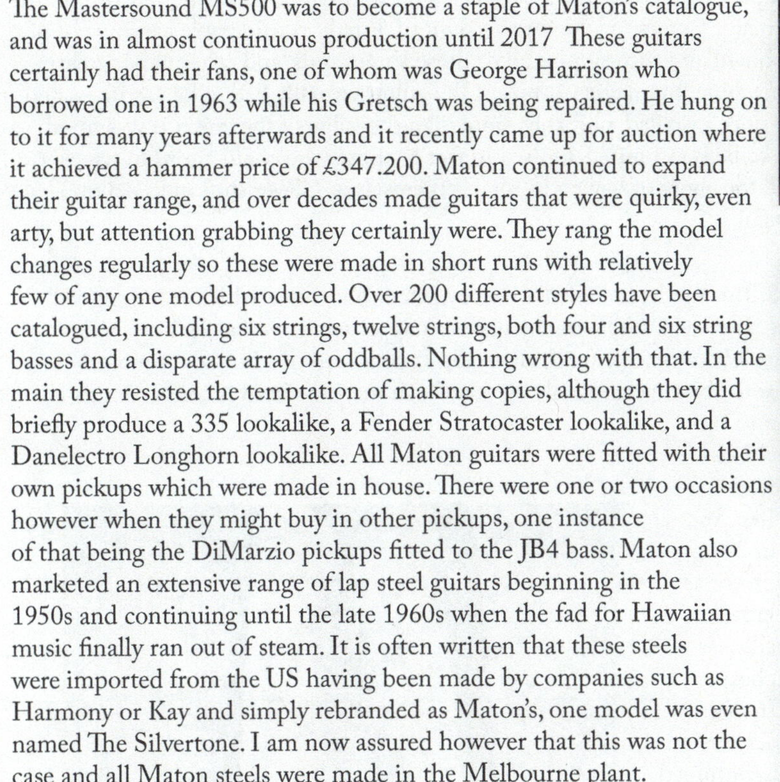

The Mastersound MS500 was to become a staple of Maton's catalogue, and was in almost continuous production until 2017 These guitars certainly had their fans, one of whom was George Harrison who borrowed one in 1963 while his Gretsch was being repaired. He hung on to it for many years afterwards and it recently came up for auction where it achieved a hammer price of £347.200. Maton continued to expand their guitar range, and over decades made guitars that were quirky, even arty, but attention grabbing they certainly were. They rang the model changes regularly so these were made in short runs with relatively few of any one model produced. Over 200 different styles have been catalogued, including six strings, twelve strings, both four and six string basses and a disparate array of oddballs. Nothing wrong with that. In the main they resisted the temptation of making copies, although they did briefly produce a 335 lookalike, a Fender Stratocaster lookalike, and a Danelectro Longhorn lookalike. All Maton guitars were fitted with their own pickups which were made in house. There were one or two occasions however when they might buy in other pickups, one instance of that being the DiMarzio pickups fitted to the JB4 bass. Maton also marketed an extensive range of lap steel guitars beginning in the 1950s and continuing until the late 1960s when the fad for Hawaiian music finally ran out of steam. It is often written that these steels were imported from the US having been made by companies such as Harmony or Kay and simply rebranded as Maton's, one model was even named The Silvertone. I am now assured however that this was not the case and all Maton steels were made in the Melbourne plant.

The Supereme

The Starline

Maton took the decision to discontinue electric guitar production in the late 1980s and focus their attention on their range of quality acoustic guitars, which by this time were attracting international attention, bolstered by the prominence of guitar virtuoso Tommy Emmanuel who favoured the brand. However times change, market swing back and forth, and Maton decided to reintroduce a range of electrics in 1998. It appears however that public interest was lukewarm, and electrics were soon dropped yet again, the final instruments being made during the covid pandemic.

The Scorpion

The aforementioned Rob Marsh tells me that a new range of solid body electrics is due for a launch very soon, and in fact, by the time you read this those new models will likely be available.

Bill May passed away in 1993. The company continues to operate, now being run by Bill's direct descendants and a team of skilled and dedicated instrument makers working at their current factory in Box Hill, a Melbourne suburb. It has to be said that Maton guitars aren't cheap. and sit comfortably mid market. Bill's emphasis on quality however hasn't been diluted, and a Maton will hold its own favourably against any other guitar in the world.

thanks to Rob Marsh at Maton

ROBOT GUITAR TUNERS

What with all the startling advances in guitar technology wouldn't it be fantastic if somebody invented a guitar that would tune itself? Well actually somebody did, more than once in fact. A simple sounding idea but the mechanics involved in making it work in a practical and efficient way proved to be a challenge.

The first such auto-tuning system that I am aware of hit the market in the early 2000s. It was known as the Transperformance System. The fitting of the unit involved removing the existing bridge and tailpiece assemblies from the guitar, whether that might have been a Les Paul or a Telecaster, both primary candidates due to their body depth, and fitting the unit in the newly created space. It was worked by a battery powered computer built into the body of the guitar which operated a series of shafts and cams pulling or releasing the string tension across the bridge. It had an onboard control panel but could also be operated by an optional footswitch. It certainly worked, various big name players owning one, but there were major factors to take into account of. Firstly, considerable carving out of the guitars body was necessary to house the computer motherboard and battery, plus all of those shafts, rods, and other moving parts. Also, those mechanics looked like the underside of a pinball machine. In practice, it meant the guitar virtually had to be sacrificed and its future value would be severely degraded. It also cost $3000 once installed, probably more than the value of the guitar it was fitted to. The potential market for these devices therefore transpired to be very limited, limited in fact to those who could afford to wreck a guitar, and to those who would spend three grand just to avoid the chore of having to tune it themselves. Clever stuff indeed, but, like so many seemingly clever widgets in this industry, doomed to fail.

The Gibson Les Paul Standard Robot guitar appeared in 2008. This model included a factory fitted robo-tuner which was designed and manufactured by a German company named Tronicaltune. They had used a totally different approach, gone to the other end of the guitar, and instead fitted their device nestled in the headstock between the machine heads. It consisted of a box containing the computer circuitry, not much bigger than a cigarette pack, powered by a rechargeable battery. Each machine head is connected to a small electric motor which receives a signal from the computer to turn one way or the other. The chip had 24 presets, and a player could also dial in his or her own custom tuning. These units were also factory fitted to several other Gibson models, SG Standards, and the like. The Robot guitar, never an outstanding success, was discontinued in 2011. Gibson also marketed these tuners under the brand name of Gforce as an accessory pack so they could be retro fitted to any guitar relatively quickly and easily, though removal of the original machine heads was necessary. In 2014 they had a retail price of $299, a whole lot cheaper than three grand, and you didn't have to carve up your guitar. In due course single side headstock fittings became available, and a bass version was also mooted. The Gibson branded units have long been discontinued but Tronicaltune continue to sell these under their own brand name. The basic idea is a brilliant one, so it's a bit of a mystery why they didn't prove to be more universally popular. You'd think that everyone would have one by now, but that's very far from the reality. I've never had one myself because I've never felt the need for one. Perhaps there's your answer.

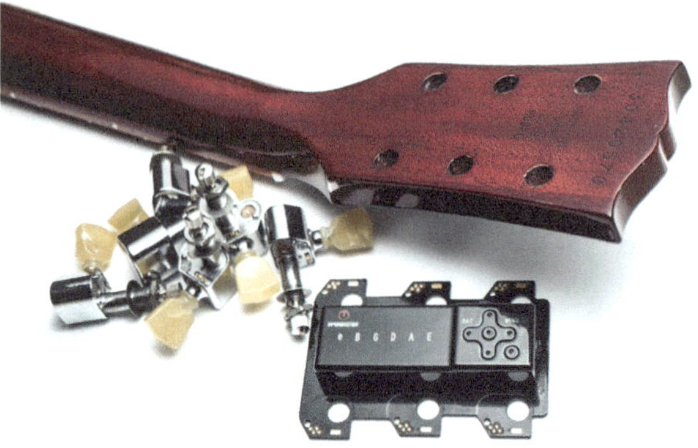

2008 Gibson V1 Robot SG Special

thanks to Imperial ~ Vintage Guitars

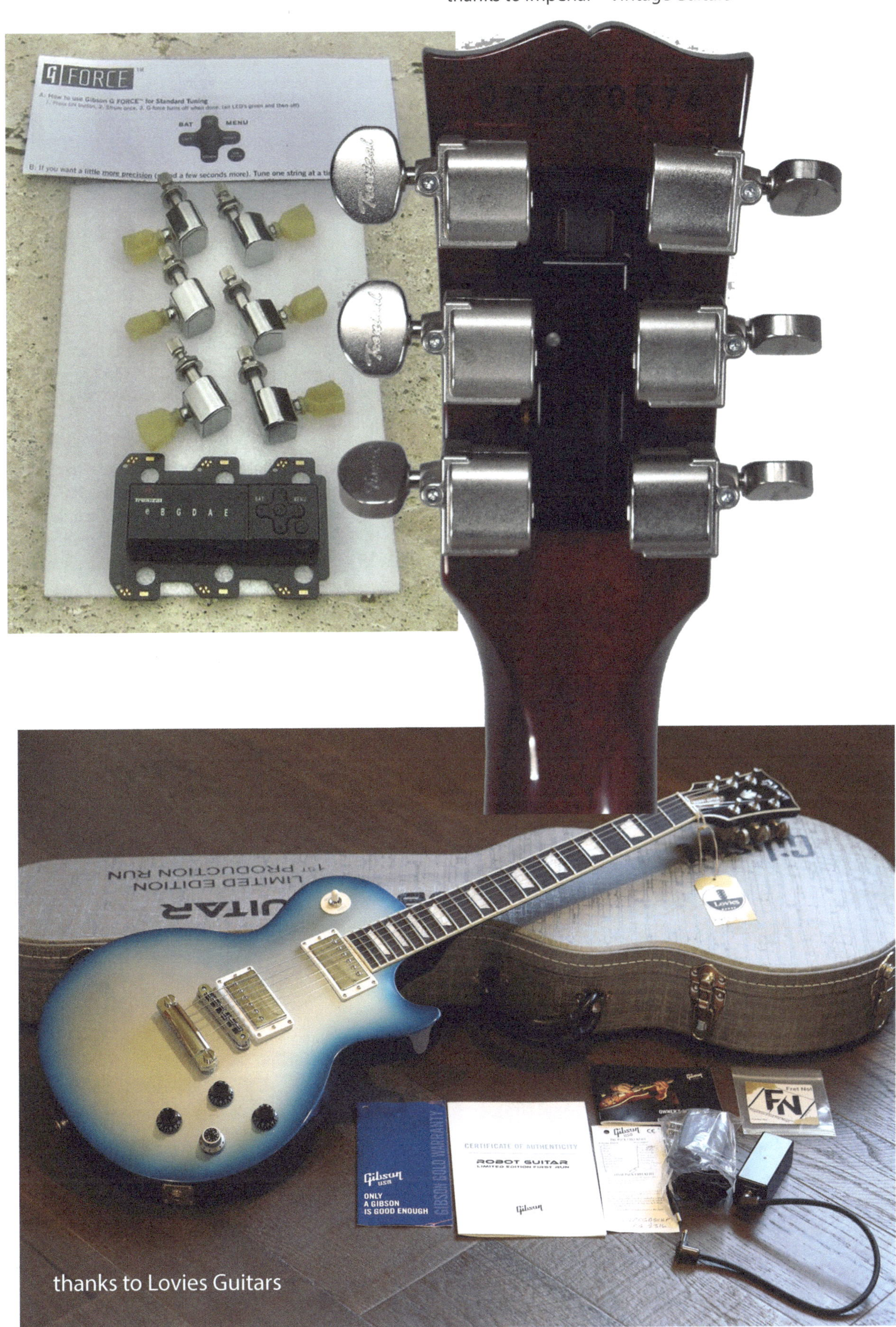

thanks to Lovies Guitars

CONTI GUITARS

Conti
GUITARS

Suppose that if I were to suggest to you that if a guitar manufacturer were to source parts and raw materials from a variety of nations spread across the world, something that would have been virtually out of the question a century ago, collect them all together in one factory, and then produce fine quality guitars as a result you might well think that this writer should seriously question his grip on reality. That however is something that Robert Conti set out to do. Jazz guitars by their very nature are expensive to manufacture when compared to solid bodies. Conti was very aware of this and determined to make quality archtop guitars available for himself, his students, and others. at far more accessible prices than some of the market leaders. Robert Conti was, and is, a jazz guitarist who enjoys a considerable degree of fame.

He was a child prodigy, turning pro at the age of 14, and mentored by the legendary Pat Martino. He is also a teacher and there are many videos of his lessons currently available on-line, DVDs too. Following a visit to the NAMM show in the early 2000s it became apparent to him that it would be practical to do exactly what I've described. He met up with manufacturers who would supply unfinished necks from Eastern Europe, premium quality ebony from either India or Cameroon, hardware from Japan, and raw bodies from South Korea. All of these components were to be assembled and finished at the factory of a company he'd made contact with at the same shows. Conti guitars were born, and the company have produced different models over the past couple of decades but currently on offer are two models, the Entrada and the Heirloom. The Entrada (Spanish for Way in I believe) is a single cutaway arch top f-hole style jazz guitar, but is ultra slim, being just 1.73 inches deep at the rim, just a whisker less than the 1.75 inches of a Gibson ES335. It has a laminated top, and the Heirloom has a carved top, but is broadly similar in all other respects. Both guitars are equipped with a single Kent Armstrong humbucker though double pickup versions are available to order at an extra cost. One interesting feature that I spotted was the so-called Goldfinger tailpiece. This is a frequensator unit but with six prongs, one for each string with a fine tuner on each prong. The only other guitar I've seen fitted with such a unit was the Bruce Bolen designed Gibson Howard Roberts Fusion from 1979, though I'm sure there have been a couple more that I haven't come across. Conti will also supply their guitars fitted with a more conventional ebony tailpiece if required. Both guitars are priced very competitively indeed in fact at the time of writing (September 2024) even the Heirloom is less than $3k, extraordinary for a carved top made in North America, and the key, in part, is due to the sourcing of components from the most economical areas of the world. I have to wonder if the same business model catches on more widely and we will see more of this in the coming years. Is this the beginning of globalisation in the guitar industry?

If you've been paying attention you might have noticed that I've barely mentioned Japanese guitars, and if at all only in passing. The Japanese, being an inventive nation, especially when it came to anything related to electronics, weren't slow out of the starting gate when it came to making electric guitars. The Guyatone brand was the first to appear, making Hawaiian style lap steels as early as 1933. These were sold principally within Japan mostly under the brand of Guya. Production of conventional electric guitars didn't commence until shortly before WWII, at which point any further development ceased. Following the war things slowly got back into gear for the country, and by 1946 Guyatone's spin off company Teisco began to make electrics in substantial quantities. Post war export restrictions meant that no guitars were shipped to Western markets until well into the '50s as far as I have been able to establish. My own first encounter with Japanese guitars wasn't until the '60s, by which time most music stores were stocking them as a cheaper alternative to Hofners, Hagstroms, and the like, plus the occasional American made guitar that showed up. I have to say for the most part that quality wise they were dire, although there were some exceptions. I certainly now recall the Guyatone brand, Terada, Antoria, Aria, and Teisco, and yet other cheaper guitars that were sold in Woolworth stores, usually under the brand names of Zenta or Satellite. What we might now refer to as the big Japanese invasion, for want of a better word, began in earnest in the '70s, and we began to see guitars bearing any one of dozens of brand names, almost all of which were copies of well known American guitars. Cheap they undeniably were, and often of poor quality, but they gave many a young buck his or her start on their lifelong guitar journey. By the end of that decade overall quality was improving and one would have had a wider choice at the entry level end, which by now included Ibanez, Yamaha and Tokai amongst others. What the Japanese were doing was crystal clear, they were mass producing what were, for the most part, cheap copies of pricey US made originals. Some were dead ringers. like some of the Tokai, whilst others were a bit half-hearted and looked it. They were able to do that as labour costs in Japan, plus raw material costs, and even the costs related to factory premises were much less than in any comparable Western country. In due course, brands such as Ibanez (Hoshino) began to market their own designs and improve quality. By the '80s players were buying Ibanez, ESP, and Yamaha guitars simply because they were good guitars in their own right, and quality had increased by light years compared to what had been coming out of Japan just a decade earlier. However, as all of those manufacturing costs increased in Japan, just as they did everywhere else, a large chunk of output was moved offshore, initially to Taiwan, later on to South Korea, and latterly to China, and even Vietnam and Indonesia, such is the ongoing battle to produce an affordable product. Things have now come full circle, and the Japanese factories that now exist are making, by any standard, quality instruments, and no longer simply cheap copies. Some in fact are very expensive and comparable to the current prices of the American brands that not so long ago they were trying hard to emulate. How times have changed. Don't panic though, all you cash-strapped beginners, you can still get started on a cheap guitar, they're just not made in Japan anymore, but in one of those other Asian countries. The overall quality is much better than it used to be too, certainly vastly better than what I could get when I was 15.

So in conclusion to all of that, I haven't covered Japanese guitars simply because I don't feel that they came up with anything new, or invented anything of significance that advanced the development or evolution of the electric guitar. They just regurgitated what was already there, though I suspect what I have said here will elicit some heated debate among you. The Japanese though did inadvertently make one significant contribution to our story, they were responsible for placing guitars into the hungry hands of starry eyed beginners who otherwise may not have been able to afford one. Some of those one-time beginners became legendary names, and for that, my friends, we should be forever grateful.

thanks to Derek Bruneau

thanks to Jim Hilmar

Tokai

Ibanez

Duesenberg

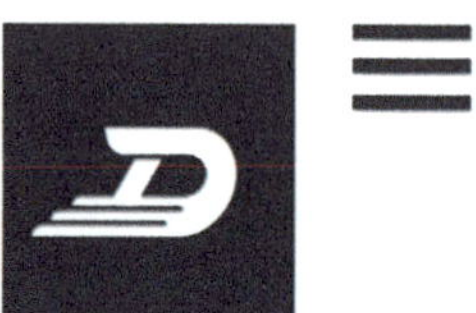

Germany has been a focus for musical instrument makers for centuries, violins, guitars, and other stringed instruments having been made in that country since at least the 1600s. Indeed there are several modern day iconic American guitar makers who can trace their origins back to old Germany, and their reputation for high quality instruments crafted from wood is well deserved. We return there now to examine one of Germany's current brands, that of Duesenberg, and to the city of Hanover.

Dieter Golsdorf had been making and selling guitars since the late '70s, under the aegis of his company Goldo Music GMBH. By 1986 he had consolidated his company, and his sporadic guitar output, into a brand, and the name he chose was Duesenberg. Whether this name was chosen as a tribute to the long defunct American auto company of the same name, who reputedly made the best cars in the world, or whether it was pure coincidence, is unclear.

His first Duesenberg brand guitars appeared in 1986. In order to mitigate costs the necks and bodies were made in Croatia and shipped to Germany for assembly and finishing, which somewhat negates the complimentary comments I made about German craftsmanship. Between '86 and '89 they primarily produced guitars for the heavy metal market, most of which had very exuberant body shapes. Finding that genre of music cooling down by the end of that decade the company resorted to more conservative body styles, and newer models included the single cut Julietta and Fantom. These were chambered solid bodies but the company's staple became the Starplayer, which was a slimline f-hole semi acoustic. There are a number of model variations, one of which is an upgraded deluxe version of the Starplayer introduced in 1995 which features Art Deco styling, lots of angles and corners, and something quite unique in guitar design. In 2002 they brought out a Ron Wood signature model, he being one of several famous users of the brand. There once was a Dave Stewart Blackbird model also.

Duesenberg make all of their own pickups including the JD-63 which I will return to in a moment. Also made in house is their Diamond Deluxe Tremola unit. Its evolution from a Bigsby unit is clear, but Duesenberg have improved the basic design, with nylon bearings and better string mountings. They also make a range of effects pedals, and their own line of amplifiers. Another noted user is Johnny Depp, and an endorsed model was released which was made to his specifications. It has a single cut chambered body, and features one of their JD-63 pickups. The surface of the guitar is covered by an aluminum plate which is engraved with reproductions of Johnny's favourite tattoos. The overall appearance is somewhat reminiscent of a Zemaitis guitar from the 70's.

Johnny Depp

Duesenberg guitars aren't exactly cheap, and in Europe, where I live, the cheapest model, listing at a whisker under 2000 euros, just about mid price, and the most expensive comes in at just under 4000 euros, putting it firmly into expensive territory.

In 2004 Duesenberg opened a production facility in Fullerton California. Here they make their Fullerton series models, which currently consist of various double cutaway semi acoustics. The TV series are available in two body sizes, all featuring a centre block and a CC series which has a deeper body. The overall quality of Duesenberg guitars is impressive, though design-wise I wouldn't say that they are innovative or have added any great leaps forward in design generally. They have though managed to supercharge certain features, especially relating to hardware and electronics, which have been around for decades, and that's not a bad thing.

Starplayer

Tom Bukovac - Wacken, 2022
copyright - Frank Schwichtenberg

MAGNATONE

The Magnatone company dates back to 1937, only nine years shy of the coverage of this book, but it wasn't always known by that name. Back then it was the Dickerson Musical Instrument Company. They traded, and made products, under the name of Magna Electronics. Due to the craze at the time for Hawaiian music, and the lap steel guitars that went along with it, a subject we have discussed before in these pages, they made a range of such instruments and their accompanying amplifiers. They also produced the same products under license for other companies. Their lap steel models had names such as the Troubadour and the Melodica. They also made an amp-in-case model very much like the Silvertone examined earlier in this book. In the early 1940s, the company was sold to the Gaston Fator Guitar Studios, but was sold yet again in 1946 to Art Duhamel, and it was he who came up with the slightly catchier name of Magnatone. That brand of amplifier proved to be very popular, being used by several big stars through the '50s. including Buddy Holly, and on into the '60s by Lonnie Mack. Many models of Magnatone amp feature a vibrato system that was patented in 1961 by electronics engineer Don Bonham. It has to be understood that a vibrato alters the pitch of a note, and is distinct from the tremolo feature found on Fenders and many other amps which only varys the volume. To the best of my knowledge the Magnatone remains the only amp with this built in piece of electronic trickery.

As the interest in the Hawaiian lap steel diminished Magnatone saw a way to expand into conventional electric Spanish guitars and employed Paul Bigsby between 1955 and 1957 to provide them with some guidance, which he did. Over time, and throughout the '50s and the '60s they made a number of different models including solid bodies such as their Zephyr, Typhoon, and Starstream. Practical workhorse guitars but nothing that would make you gasp in amazement. They also made a guitar christened the Mk V, which was surprisingly akin to a late '50s double cutaway Gibson Melody Maker. Some thin-line semi acoustics were also part of the range by the mid '60s, taking advantage of public demand for such things in the wake of the early '60s British Beat Boom. One series of models gave us these rather cheeky Rickenbacker copies which can be seen here. Rickenbacker, as is well known, have a zero tolerance to anybody stealing their designs. and old Mr. F C Hall must have had an apoplectic fit when he saw those. Rickenbacker immediately issued Magnatone with a strongly worded Cease and Desist letter, threatening litigation of they didn't comply, and Magnatone wisely backed down. They were not in a strong enough position by this time anyway to be able to afford an expensive court case and one they would certainly lose. Amplifier production continued, but by this time new solid state amplifiers were beginning to appear. They were lighter and easier to carry around, cheaper to make, and intrinsically more reliable. Despite the fact that early examples of transistor amps sounded pretty horrible they were selling, and the sales of conventional tube amps were falling off a cliff, a fact not helped by having to compete in an overcrowded market. By the late '60s, the company's financial position had become precarious. With the hope of making a last ditch cost saving stratagem to rescue the company they moved the factory to the small but aptly named town of Harmony in southern Minnesota. This was a small town indeed with a population of barely 1000 and incidentally home to the largest Amish community in the Midwest. Not my first choice for an amplifier factory, and it was at this juncture that most of the key employees departed, not wishing to exchange the Southern California climate for the brutal Minnesotan winters. The relocation didn't produce the desired result unfortunately, the final outcome being that the company went insolvent in 1969.

The Magnatone brand name became moribund and passed into obscurity, for a while at least. The marque was purchased in 2013 by Ted Kornblum, an ex Ampeg employee. He had a vision of building limited numbers of what essentially were boutique amps harking back to the good old days of craftsman built, hand wired amps, point to point wiring (whatever that means), and just like amps used to be, EL34's and all. Billy F Gibbons, always a big fan of Magnatone amps, came on board to lend his expertise to design, performance, and raising their visibility to new levels after many years in the wilderness. There are currently eleven models in the range, built today in St Louis, Missouri, and they seem to be enjoying a new lease of life despite their rather high cost. As they say, in life, you get what you pay for. No more guitars just yet though.

1957 Paul Bigsby's influence

thanks to ATB Guitars

Magnatone X-20 Typhoon 1960s

thanks to fun-japanproduct

CORAL GUITARS

Coral

Coral was a short lived range of guitars, effectively a spin-off from Danelectro. When Danelectro was purchased by the Music Corporation of America in 1966, MCA launched the Coral line, though still produced in the Danelectro factory, but, it was hoped, a more modern approach to a more modern market. The range consisted of basses, bearing a strong resemblance to Fender's offset contour models such as the Jazzmaster and Jaguar, but are best remembered now by their extraordinary electric sitar, designed by session guitarist Vincent Bell. This arrived at exactly the right time to cash in on the hippie movement and an interest in sounds of an eastern origin. No great numbers of these were made hence they fetch high prices in the collectors market these days. Vincent Bell is also known for his Bellzouki, a teardrop shaped 12 string, loosely based on the design of a traditional Greek bouzouki. This bore the Danelectro brand and allegedly was produced from 1961 to 1968. Danelectro ceased operations in 1969 and I can't find any evidence that the Coral name survived beyond this date.

thanks to Dave D'Amelio and Drowning in Guitars

JAZZ GUITARS TODAY

When I was still a young lad, in about 1960 or '61, and just starting on my path, I listened avidly to my dad's Django Reinhardt and Les Paul records. I also listened to other jazz greats like Herb Ellis, Johnny Smith, Kenny Burrell, and others. Once I'd heard that sublime tone I was hooked. I was once standing in a guitar shop ogling guitars I couldn't possibly afford, when I, by chance, met another guitarist, far older and more experienced than I. He must have sensed my enthusiasm so we chatted about guitars and the future, and he imparted to me this pearl of wisdom, "You could be playing 5000 chords to three people, or you could be playing three chords to 5000 people. Your choice". Within the week I had joined a rock and roll band. A dilemma I suspect many guitar players have had to wrestle with.

Since the 1950's and the dominance of rock n roll, and other genres of popular music, the jazz guitarists seem to have been elbowed out of the limelight following their heyday in the '30s and '40s. Popular interest in any style of music waxes and wanes, that's only to be expected, but, and especially during the '70s and '80s, the jazzers seem to have retreated into the realm of niche music, listened to by just an often small cabal of dedicated fans. So it appears that the guy in the guitar shop had been right, up to a point anyway. It seems to be the case though that there has been a resurgence of the style over the past couple of decades. The overall picture as far as manufacturers are concerned has been patchy. It is true that some makers, such as Guild, Heritage, and Epiphone, still feature full bodied jazz guitars in their ranges, whereas Gibson have all but eliminated theirs, and that gorgeous Rickenbacker 390 is also, sadly, no more, (John Hall, if you are reading this, please make some more). As remarked on earlier Stromberg are still making such things, as are D'Angelico, who are making a range of archtop guitars in the Far East. The Eastman company are also offering a few, and emanating from the same source. Paradoxically perhaps there has been a noticeable increase in custom builders, Benedetto being one more famous example. D'Aquisto was another, though he sadly died in 1996. Some prime examples are pictured on the adjoining page. So jazz guitarists, and the tools of their trade, never went away, they were there all the time. Most of us just never noticed. Frank Zappa once said, "If you want to learn to play guitar just buy yourself a Wes Montgomery record". I'll go along with that.

Benedetto.
Fibonacci
Peerless
Archtop&Acousticguitars
Epiphone
Ibanez

The evolution of Fender and Gibson has been the most significant factor in the history of the electric guitar. The USA led the world in design and construction with many fine technical and managerial minds working together. The Stratocaster, Les Paul Standard, Gibson ES, and Telecaster became household names. After 75 years these guitars are still considered the most successful designs and are still sought after by young and old players. Fender in particular has done a lot of work on marketing across genders increasing their market share. There have been many changes in ownership which we have mentioned, some detrimental, and others creating a positive direction. In a world of technology and obsolescence, it is strange that most of the manufacturers are still trying to recreate the guitars from the original designs and the Custom Shops turn out a huge number of vintage re-issues.

In the '80s Fender were the first to realise the potential of 'Artist' models, and we can thank the work of John Hill who helped re-structure the Fender company, working with Dan Smith, focusing on the British Isles based guitarists he was already working with. Hill established the first Fender Artist Relations office in the world in London and later also brought Gibson from Nashville to London establishing The Gibson Garage. Following the Fender Management buyout from CBS in 1985, Hill and Smith approached Eric Clapton about a signature model. Hill had already been supplying Jeff Beck with critically selected Strats since 1980 towards custom prototypes and with David Gilmour since '83 and his 'The Red Strat' and 'Cream No 2' emerged from these sorties. Fender said no to Signatures as they said it was a Gibson thing, and apart from the Les Paul, Gibson didn't sell many, but Hill had many major British guitarists waiting in the wings. It would be Fender's mission to make the finest guitars in the world in the USA and get back to the consistent levels of quality and innovation of Leo Fender's golden era. Hill began discussing and speccing what became the EC Signature with Eric and in the process was able to sell the idea of signature models to Fender. The resulting EC signature Strat equipped with Lace Sensor pickups and active mid boost system, appeared in the stores in 1988 creating a huge impact. This was the start of a long line of artist models and together with the Custom Shop, Fender were never so successful.

Today we have Fender with direct sales to customers on the internet and customer designed specs, flagship stores opening and the big retailers collaborating directly with the company specified designs. Fender has a plant in Mexico where their best selling models can be made at lower cost with great quality. The changing political landscape may change this price advantage in the States at any time, although the rest of the world will still benefit from some finely built and sounding guitars.

The first post-CBS Strat along with David Gilmour, Eric Clapton, Hank Marvin and Jeff Beck. They discuss the proposal, for a working partnership, producing Artist guitars. The first of these began during the recording of Jeff Beck's There and Back album with John taking prototypes to Air Studios. They would eventually become the American Vintage Series and developed into what Hill named the Graffiti Yellow Strat for Jeff with custom trems, pups, and nut technologies. In parallel Hill was working on what became the Eric Clapton Signature Strat and the contract that he was negotiating with Roger Forrester, Eric's manager, and was a first of its kind in the MI industry. It led to adding $500m to the value of post CBS Fender and enabling Fender, Hill, and Dan Smith to rebrand Fender raising $22m to build the new Corona plant and Custom Shop expansion.

Joe Brown, Hank Marvin and Bert Weedon at the official opening of the Fender AR&D Centre in London 1987.

David Gilmour
Madison Square Garden
November 4, 2024.
'The Black Cat Strat' re-issue
thanks to
www.jamesliverani.com

this feature was created with the help of John Hill

thanks to Mufasa Shu

GIBSON GUITARS TODAY

Pat presenting Jimmy with the Zosa LP at the last Riffathon event.

Gibson were a little later than Fender in getting into the modern Artist series. Their earlier success as a company was due in part to the Gibson 'All Stars' featured in the 1950s catalogues. The motivator in the '90s was Pat Foley who was working for the company in London. He was a friend of Jimmy Page and, in short, they came up with the proposal to copy the famous No.1 Les Paul Standard. Pat was then appointed Artist Relations Manager and was behind the success of the Artist and Collectors Choice series. The work of Pat Foley and Edward Wilson will be remembered as the 'Golden Years' of Gibson and their work continued with the Heritage, 60th Anniversary, and Murphy Lab guitars

The Gibson Garage opened in 2021 in Nashville with the London Garage following in 2023. These stores follow the concept of the Apple flagship stores where major companies promote their own brand. Very hi-tech design and packed with the latest models, special issues, and events - the Garage is a consumer experience.

Gibson and Pat instigated the Montserrat concert in 1997. Pat had a close family and working relationship with Sir George Martin. When approached, George immediately phoned the stellar cast of performers, who readily accepted to take part in the charity concert.

With artists such as Jimmy Page, Billy Gibbons, Slash, Peter Green, and Gary Moore there is a huge market re-issuing the classic guitars of the golden years. The Gibson Garage hosts special events to promote the release of these iconic re-issues.

Richard Fortus Collection

Slash first Burst - 1958
Artist proof No.4

Mufasa Shu

AND WHAT OF THE FUTURE!

In these pages, we have watched the electric guitar being invented, developed, and endlessly tweaked until it evolved finally into the artifact we see and enjoy so much now. It is however just that, evolution, and it hasn't ended yet. The popularity of the instrument ebbs and flows, and that popularity, and resultant sales potential, are driven very much by the age in which it exists. The advent of rock and roll saw it take off, its visibility increased during the surfing and instrumental group years, and its presence cemented for good once the Beatles, Stones, and all those other guitar, bass, and drum bands appeared in the '60s. That period was followed by the rise of heavier guitar led rock groups, Free, Grateful Dead, Steppenwolf, Ted Nugent, Mountain, Cream, Whitesnake, Blue Oyster Cult, Led Zep and the rest where guitar was king, and the players Gods.

Everything however must pass and the world moves on. By the late '70s things were noticeably starting to lose traction somewhat. As I stated earlier guitar sales had peaked in '77 and it was downhill from there. I was working in the guitar retail trade at the time, and one poor quarter was followed by another poor quarter and by '78 it was decided that our shop would close. Several other shops in the area followed suit. The gold rush was over, for now at least. Guitar led rock music lost its momentum and during the '80s was replaced by electropop and synth pop, hardly a guitar to be seen, and as guitar sales were primarily driven by what was happening in popular music generally sales slumped, and that would be the case for the next couple of decades. There were bands who managed to keep the ball rolling, AC/DC, Metallica, and those dear old chaps in the Rolling Stones, but for most, it was either game over or the oldies circuit. That state of affairs trickled right through to the manufacturers. Some experienced financial difficulties but somehow survived, others didn't survive and went to the wall, and others managed to hang on by moving most if not all, production to the Far East where instruments could be made more cheaply. That said there were new start-ups too, such as PRS in '85, and Parker in '93, There was life in that old guitar yet. By 2000, and according to industry stats, things were picking up. As the next couple of decades passed sales grew steadily, driven not so much by bands, or by popular music trends, but by individuals who saw the guitar as a hobby, a lifestyle choice, and one that was both creative and rewarding. It surprised me to learn that out of new starters in 2010 the average age was 30, and 49% were female. Sales wise, and according to yet more stats 1.6 million guitars were sold globally in 2015, and by 2023 that figure had increased to 2.6 million. The exact figures given as statistics on a variety of websites during my research varied considerably, but the one thing that was common throughout was a distinct upward trend. Those figures of course are for all guitars, classical nylon strung acoustics, steel strung acoustics, and electrics. Most list an average spend of between 400 USD and 500 USD, but if you take acoustics out of the equation the average spend on an electric is currently around 1000 USD. There was incidentally a big spike in the figures during the recent covid pandemic. People who were forced to remain inside for long periods and were seeking something to occupy their spare time found that their long dreamt of desire to learn to play the guitar could finally become a reality, so they went online and bought one. Britain's largest on-line retailer Gear4Music reported that 2019 had been their best year ever. As far as guitars are directly concerned the old favourites remain popular, notwithstanding the fact that they were designed 60 or 70 years ago, so it's still all about Stratocasters, Telecasters, SGs, Les Pauls, 335s and so on. There will inevitably be a younger crowd who don't care about names or history, but who are looking for something new and different, more in line with today's technological culture, and that's the way it should be. Carbon fiber guitars have been around for a while, but various companies are experimenting with newer plastics and polymers, so guitars can be made lighter, more resonant, and more cheaply. We are also seeing instruments that can be interfaced with laptops and other devices that contain software to aid the learning process or to help with composition and home recordings. Smart guitars are on the way and are being developed as I write this. AI guitars will be next. Please don't ask me how those will work. I'm very much old school. Just give me a guitar, plug me into an amp as big as a bus and I'll be happy with that.

If I've mistakenly skipped over your personal favourite, or if you happen to work for a company that doesn't appear here, then I send you my sincerest apologies. One hundred years is a very long time. All of those legendary names that been mentioned in these pages who launched this instrument on its journey are gone now, and their milestones have become tombstones. As generations pass from one to the next new kids on the block will emerge, bringing with them new inventions and innovations, even occasional flashes of brilliance, so the story will continue. I forecast that in 2128 someone will write a book entitled Two Centuries Of The Electric Guitar, but I know it won't be me.

We leave you with what is probably the finest designed guitar to emerge from the 1950s. It certainly had a huge impact on the guitar world With guitarists such as Buddy Holly, Eric Clapton, Jeff Beck, Jimi Hendrix, and David Gilmour all using it with such great effect the Fender Stratocaster was a masterpiece. It remains as one of the most popular guitars of all time.

We thank you for sharing this book and hope you have found it interesting and a fun read

Sid and David

R.I.P.

We offer this as a memorial to all of those great guitar players who are no longer with us. The list is comprised of over one hundred and fifty names, it is a tragically long list, and I'm fairly confident it merely scratches the surface, so my sincere apologies if I've missed a few. Some were cruelly taken at a young age, their flames burning only briefly, though it has to be said some were victims of their unwise lifestyle choices. Others lived long productive lives, and all possible stages in between. They all leave behind them, not just memories, but large bodies of work which can be appreciated and enjoyed by all of us for decades to come. The one thing that links them all is their proficiency in their chosen instrument, the electric guitar, in my view the most expressive of all musical instruments, capable of an infinite sonic soundscape, and they all should be recognized for the contribution that each and every one of them made to the visibility and present day prominence of the guitar. Sadly then these are our fallen heroes. We salute them and will remember them. As Keith Richards once said, "The guitar is a harsh mistress". So, in no particular order.

Duane Eddy, Carl Perkins, Link Wray, David Crosby, Muddy Waters, Elmore James, Chuck Berry, Dickey Betts, Bo Diddley, Ike Turner, Charlie Christian, Alan Murphy (Kate Bush Band), Johnny Winter, Lonnie Mack, Lowell Fulson, Erik Brann (Iron Butterfly), Jeff Healey, Jimi Hendrix, Jerry Garcia, Paul Kossoff, Al 'Blind Owl' Wilson (Canned Heat), Leslie West, Robbie Robertson, Randy California, Lou Reed, Tom Fogerty (Creedence Clearwater Revival), George Harrison John Lennon, Martin Stone (The Action), Top Topham (Yardbirds), Carl Wilson (Beach Boys), Terry Kath (Chicago), Wes Montgomery, Allen Collins (Lynyrd Skynyrd), Django Reinhardt, Marc Bolan, Dan Armstrong, J J Cale, Jimmy McCullogh (Wings), Clarence White, Glenn Schwartz (Pacific Gas And Electric), John Cippolina (Quicksilver Messenger Service), Gary Duncan (Quicksilver Messenger Service), Johnny Smith, Larry Coryell, Hank Garland, Glen Campbell, Steve Gaines (Lynyrd Skynyrd), Ian Bairnson (Kate Bush Band), Herb Ellis, Les Paul, Ike Isaacs, Amancio D'Silva, Jim Hall, "Dimebag Darrell" Abbott, Glen, Buxton (Alice Cooper), Kurt Cobain, Prince, Eddie, Van Halen, Matt Guitar Murphy, Arbee Stidham, Homesick James, Hubert Sumlin, Howlin' Wolf, Cliff Gallup, Eddie Cochran, Bucky Pizzarelli, Billy Byrd, Glenn Frey, Tommy DeVito (Four Seasons), Jack Lathrop (Glenn Miller Orchestra), Freddie Green (Count Basie Orchestra), Francis 'Franny' Beecher (Bill Haley's Comets), Albert King, Brian Jones, Steve Clark (Def Leppard), Gary Moore, Alvin Lee (Ten Years After), Albert Collins, B B King, Luther Allison, Stevie Ray Vaughan, Ronnie Montrose, Frank Zappa, Dave Ball (Procol Harum), Dick Dale, Randy Rhoads, Malcolm Young (AC/DC), George Young (Easybeats), Shawn Lane (Black Oak Arkansas), Dave Brock (Hawkwind), Tommy Bolin, Jeff Hanneman (Slayer), Wilko Johnson (Dr Feelgood), Jimmy Reed, Duane Allman, Mike Bloomfield, Mark Moffatt, Tito Jackson, Paul Brett, Howard Roberts, Tony Peluso (Carpenters), Tommy Tedesco, Vic Flick, Clarence Gatemouth Brown, Martin Jenner (Cliff Richard Band), Mick Ronson (David Bowie), Big Jim Sullivan, Jeff Beck, Vinnie Taylor (Sha Na Na), Danny McBride (Sha Na Na), Chris Cornell, Freddie King, Luther "Guitar Junior" Johnson, Lowell George (Little Feat), Bob Bogle (Ventures), Duster Bennett, Tony McPhee (Groundhogs), Allan Holdsworth, Ivor Mairants (Ted Heath Orchestra), Dave Goldberg (Ted Heath Orchestra), Hilton Valentine (Animals), Bert Weedon, Bernie Marsden (Whitesnake), Sister Rosetta Tharpe, Alexis Korner, Huw Lloyd-Langton (Hawkwind), Johnny Thunders (New York Dolls), T Bone Walker, Chet Atkins, Slim Harpo, John Lee Hooker, Sal Salvador, Larry Collins, James Honeyman-Scott (Pretenders), Scotty Moore, Merle Travis, George Van Eps, Roy Clark (He-Haw), Syd Barrett (Pink Floyd), Johnny Ramone, Rick Parfitt (StatusQuo), Steve Marriott, Kim Simmonds (Savoy Brown), Les Harvey (Stone The Crows), Danny Kirwan (Fleetwood Mac), Ron Asheton (The Stooges), Wayne Kramer (MC5), Alvino Rey, John Mayall, Mary Osborne, Mary Ford, Pat Martino, George Barnes, Danny Cedrone (Bill Haley), Nick Lucas

and now for some earthshaking bass players

Dickie Peterson (Blue Cheer), Jack Bruce, Felix Papallardi, John Entwistle, Jaco Pastorius, Noel Redding, Alan Rogan (Prelude), Jet Harris'(Shadows), John Rostill (Shadows), Pete Farndon (Pretenders), Dusty Hill, Phil Lynott (Thin Lizzy), Andy Fraser (Free), Alan Lancaster (Status Quo), Duncan Sanderson (Deviants), Randy Meisner, Chas Chandler (Animals), Ronnie Lane (Faces), Heinz Burt (Tornados), Dee Dee Ramone, Jerry Miller (Moby Grape), Mo Foster, Herbie Flowers, Phil Lesh (Grateful Dead). Tim Bogert (Vanilla Fudge)

P.O. Box 17878-Anaheim Hills, CA
www.Centerstream-USA.com